Interactive Notebooks

SCIENCE

Grade 5

Credits

Author: Sara Haynes Blackwood
Content Editors: Elise Craver, Christine Schwab, Angela Triplett

Visit *carsondellosa.com* for correlations to Common Core, state, national, and Canadian provincial standards.

Carson-Dellosa Publishing LLC
PO Box 35665
Greensboro, NC 27425 USA
carsondellosa.com

978-1-4838-3125-1
06-088217784

Table of Contents

What Are Interactive Notebooks?

Interactive notebooks are a unique form of note taking. Teachers guide students through creating pages of notes on new topics. Instead of being in the traditional linear, handwritten format, notes are colorful and spread across the pages. Notes also often include drawings, diagrams, and 3-D elements to make the material understandable and relevant. Students are encouraged to complete their notebook pages in ways that make sense to them. With this personalization, no two pages are exactly the same.

Because of their creative nature, interactive notebooks allow students to be active participants in their own learning. Teachers can easily differentiate pages to address the levels and needs of each learner. The notebooks are arranged sequentially, and students can create tables of contents as they create pages, making it simple for students to use their notebooks for reference throughout the year. The interactive, easily personalized format makes interactive notebooks ideal for engaging students in learning new concepts.

Using interactive notebooks can take as much or as little time as you like. Students will initially take longer to create pages but will get faster as they become familiar with the process of creating pages. You may choose to only create a notebook page as a class at the beginning of each unit, or you may choose to create a new page for each topic within a unit. You can decide what works best for your students and schedule.

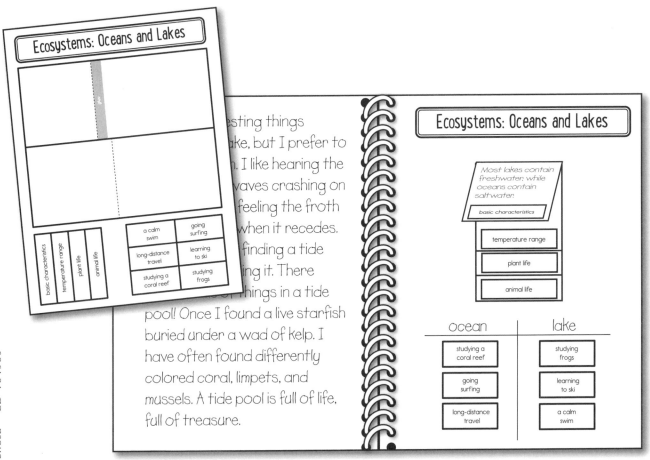

A student's interactive notebook for ocean and lake ecosystems

Getting Started

You can start using interactive notebooks at any point in the school year. Use the following guidelines to help you get started in your classroom. (For more specific details, management ideas, and tips, see page 10.)

1. Plan each notebook.

Use the planning template (page 9) to lay out a general plan for the topics you plan to cover in each notebook for the year.

2. Choose a notebook type.

Interactive notebooks are usually either single-subject, spiral-bound notebooks, composition books, or three-ring binders with loose-leaf paper. Each type presents pros and cons. See page 5 for a more in-depth look at each type of notebook.

3. Allow students to personalize their notebooks.

Have students decorate their notebook covers, as well as add their names and subjects. This provides a sense of ownership and emphasizes the personalized nature of the notebooks.

4. Number the pages and create the table of contents.

Have students number the bottom outside corner of each page, front and back. When completing a new page, adding a table of contents entry will be easy. Have students title the first page of each notebook "Table of Contents." Have them leave several blank pages at the front of each notebook for the table of contents. Refer to your general plan for an idea of about how many entries students will be creating.

5. Start creating pages.

Always begin a new page by adding an entry to the table of contents. Create the first notebook pages along with students to model proper format and expectations.

This book contains individual topics for you to introduce. Use the pages in the order that best fits your curriculum. You may also choose to alter the content presented to better match your school's curriculum. The provided lesson plans often do not instruct students to add color. Students should make their own choices about personalizing the content in ways that make sense to them. Encourage students to highlight and color the pages as they desire while creating them.

After introducing topics, you may choose to add more practice pages. Use the reproducibles (pages 78–96) to easily create new notebook pages for practice or to introduce topics not addressed in this book.

Use the grading rubric (page 11) to grade students' interactive notebooks at various points throughout the year. Provide students copies of the rubric to glue into their notebooks and refer to as they create pages.

What Type of Notebook Should I Use?

Spiral Notebook

The pages in this book are formatted for a standard one-subject notebook.

Pros

- Notebook can be folded in half.
- Page size is larger.
- It is inexpensive.
- It often comes with pockets for storing materials.

Cons

- Pages can easily fall out.
- Spirals can snag or become misshapen.
- Page count and size vary widely.
- It is not as durable as a binder.

Tips

- Encase the spiral in duct tape to make it more durable.
- Keep the notebooks in a central place to prevent them from getting damaged in desks.

Composition Notebook

Pros

- Pages don't easily fall out.
- Page size and page count are standard.
- It is inexpensive.

Cons

- Notebook cannot be folded in half.
- Page size is smaller.
- It is not as durable as a binder.

Tips

- Copy pages meant for standard-sized notebooks at 85 or 90 percent. Test to see which works better for your notebook.

Binder with Loose-Leaf Paper

Pros

- Pages can be easily added, moved, or removed.
- Pages can be removed individually for grading.
- You can add full-page printed handouts.
- It has durable covers.

Cons

- Pages can easily fall out.
- Pages aren't durable.
- It is more expensive than a notebook.
- Students can easily misplace or lose pages.
- Larger size makes it more difficult to store.

Tips

- Provide hole reinforcers for damaged pages.

How to Organize an Interactive Notebook

You may organize an interactive notebook in many different ways. You may choose to organize it by unit and work sequentially through the book. Or, you may choose to create different sections that you will revisit and add to throughout the year. Choose the format that works best for your students and subject.

An interactive notebook includes different types of pages in addition to the pages students create. Non-content pages you may want to add include the following:

Title Page

This page is useful for quickly identifying notebooks. It is especially helpful in classrooms that use multiple interactive notebooks for different subjects. Have students write the subject (such as "Science") on the title page of each interactive notebook. They should also include their full names. You may choose to have them include other information such as the teacher's name, classroom number, or class period.

Table of Contents

The table of contents is an integral part of the interactive notebook. It makes referencing previously created pages quick and easy for students. Make sure that students leave several pages at the beginning of each notebook for a table of contents.

Expectations and Grading Rubric

It is helpful for each student to have a copy of the expectations for creating interactive notebook pages. You may choose to include a list of expectations for parents and students to sign, as well as a grading rubric (page 11).

Unit Title Pages

Consider using a single page at the beginning of each section to separate it. Title the page with the unit name. Add a tab (page 78) to the edge of the page to make it easy to flip to the unit. Add a table of contents for only the pages in that unit.

Glossary

Reserve a six-page section at the back of the notebook where students can create a glossary. Draw a line to split in half the front and back of each page, creating 24 sections. Combine Q and R and Y and Z to fit the entire alphabet. Have students add an entry as each new vocabulary word is introduced.

Formatting Student Notebook Pages

The other major consideration for planning an interactive notebook is how to treat the left and right sides of a notebook spread. Interactive journals are usually viewed with the notebook open flat. This creates a left side and a right side. You have several options for how to treat the two sides of the spread.

Traditionally, the right side is used for the teacher-directed part of the lesson, and the left side is used for students to interact with the lesson content. The lessons in this book use this format. However, you may prefer to switch the order for your class so that the teacher-directed learning is on the left and the student input is on the right.

It can also be important to include standards, learning objectives, or essential questions in interactive notebooks. You may choose to write these on the top-left side of each page before completing the teacher-directed page on the right side. You may also choose to have students include the "Introduction" part of each lesson in that same top-left section. This is the *in, through, out* method. Students enter *in* the lesson on the top left of the page, go *through* the lesson on the right page, and exit *out* of the lesson on the bottom left with a reflection activity.

The following chart details different types of items and activities that you could include on each side.

Left Side Student Output	Right Side Teacher-Directed Learning
• learning objectives • essential questions • I Can statements • brainstorming • making connections • summarizing • making conclusions • practice problems • opinions • questions • mnemonics • drawings and diagrams	• vocabulary and definitions • mini-lessons • folding activities • steps in a process • example problems • notes • diagrams • graphic organizers • hints and tips • big ideas

Planning for the Year

Making a general plan for interactive notebooks will help with planning, grading, and testing throughout the year. You do not need to plan every single page, but knowing what topics you will cover and in what order can be helpful in many ways.

Use the Interactive Notebook Plan (page 9) to plan your units and topics and where they should be placed in the notebooks. Remember to include enough pages at the beginning for the non-content pages, such as the title page, table of contents, and grading rubric. You may also want to leave a page at the beginning of each unit to place a mini table of contents for just that section.

In addition, when planning new pages, it can be helpful to sketch the pieces you will need to create. Use the following notebook template and notes to plan new pages.

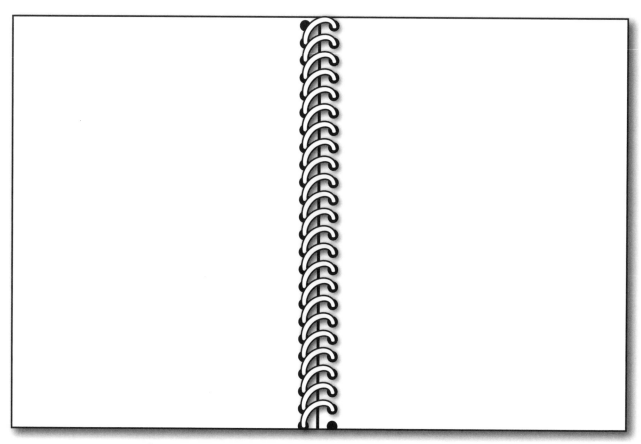

Left Side   **Right Side**

Notes

_____

_____

_____

Interactive Notebook Plan

Page	Topic	Page	Topic
1		51	
2		52	
3		53	
4		54	
5		55	
6		56	
7		57	
8		58	
9		59	
10		60	
11		61	
12		62	
13		63	
14		64	
15		65	
16		66	
17		67	
18		68	
19		69	
20		70	
21		71	
22		72	
23		73	
24		74	
25		75	
26		76	
27		77	
28		78	
29		79	
30		80	
31		81	
32		82	
33		83	
34		84	
35		85	
36		86	
37		87	
38		88	
39		89	
40		90	
41		91	
42		92	
43		93	
44		94	
45		95	
46		96	
47		97	
48		98	
49		99	
50		100	

Managing Interactive Notebooks in the Classroom

Working with Younger Students

- Use your yearly plan to preprogram a table of contents that you can copy and give to students to glue into their notebooks, instead of writing individual entries.

- Have assistants or parent volunteers precut pieces.

- Create glue sponges to make gluing easier. Place large sponges in plastic containers with white glue. The sponges will absorb the glue. Students can wipe the backs of pieces across the sponges to apply the glue with less mess.

Creating Notebook Pages

- For storing loose pieces, add a pocket to the inside back cover. Use the envelope pattern (page 81), an envelope, a jumbo library pocket, or a resealable plastic bag. Or, tape the bottom and side edges of the two last pages of the notebook together to create a large pocket.

- When writing under flaps, have students trace the outline of each flap so that they can visualize the writing boundary.

- Where the dashed line will be hidden on the inside of the fold, have students first fold the piece in the opposite direction so that they can see the dashed line. Then, students should fold the piece back the other way along the same fold line to create the fold in the correct direction.

- To avoid losing pieces, have students keep all of their scraps on their desks until they have finished each page.

- To contain paper scraps and avoid multiple trips to the trash can, provide small groups with small buckets or tubs.

- For students who run out of room, keep full and half sheets available. Students can glue these to the bottom of the pages and fold them up when not in use.

Dealing with Absences

- Create a model notebook for absent students to reference when they return to school.

- Have students cut a second set of pieces as they work on their own pages.

Using the Notebook

- To organize sections of the notebook, provide each student with a sheet of tabs (page 78).

- To easily find the next blank page, either cut off the top-right corner of each page as it is used or attach a long piece of yarn or ribbon to the back cover to be used as a bookmark.

Interactive Notebook Grading Rubric

4

_____ Table of contents is complete.

_____ All notebook pages are included.

_____ All notebook pages are complete.

_____ Notebook pages are neat and organized.

_____ Information is correct.

_____ Pages show personalization, evidence of learning, and original ideas.

3

_____ Table of contents is mostly complete.

_____ One notebook page is missing.

_____ Notebook pages are mostly complete.

_____ Notebook pages are mostly neat and organized.

_____ Information is mostly correct.

_____ Pages show some personalization, evidence of learning, and original ideas.

2

_____ Table of contents is missing a few entries.

_____ A few notebook pages are missing.

_____ A few notebook pages are incomplete.

_____ Notebook pages are somewhat messy and unorganized.

_____ Information has several errors.

_____ Pages show little personalization, evidence of learning, or original ideas.

1

_____ Table of contents is incomplete.

_____ Many notebook pages are missing.

_____ Many notebook pages are incomplete.

_____ Notebook pages are too messy and unorganized to use.

_____ Information is incorrect.

_____ Pages show no personalization, evidence of learning, or original ideas.

Ecosystems

Introduction

Before the lesson, write the word *ecosystem* on the board. Use a self-stick note to cover the letters "eco." Have students work in small groups to create definitions of the word *system*. Allow groups to share their definitions. Then, use them to create a class definition and write it on the board below the word. Remove the self-stick note. Discuss how the prefix changes the definition. Introduce the idea of an ecosystem.

Creating the Notebook Page

Guide students through the following steps to complete the right-hand page in their notebooks.

1. Add a Table of Contents entry for the Ecosystems pages.

2. Cut out the title and glue it to the top of the page.

3. Cut out the accordion piece. Fold on the dashed lines, alternating direction so that the largest section is on top. Apply glue to the back of the smallest section and attach it to the page below the title.

4. Write the name of an ecosystem, such as *Forest*, on the line in the top section. Complete the definition on each flap (Organism: a **single plant** or **animal**; Population: more than **one** of the **same plant** or **animal**; Community: all of the **living things** in the same **area**; Ecosystem: all of the **living** and **nonliving** things in the same **area**). Then, draw a picture to illustrate each term.

5. Cut out the sun flap. Apply glue to the back of the top section and attach it below the accordion fold. Under the flap, describe the importance of the sun to an ecosystem.

6. Draw arrows to the left and right of the sun flap to show the sun's role in an ecosystem. For example, draw an arrow to a green plant to show photosynthesis at work, or an arrow to a water source to show the sun's role in the water cycle.

7. Cut out the *An ecosystem consists* piece and glue it below the sun flap.

8. Discuss the two main parts of an ecosystem and complete the blanks (**living** things; **nonliving** things). Continue the vertical line straight down the page to create a T-chart.

9. Cut out the eight labels. Glue each label in the correct column on the T-chart.

Reflect on Learning

To complete the left-hand page, have students choose an ecosystem and draw a picture of it. Students should include at least five different plants and five different animals. Have students label the living and nonliving parts of the ecosystem.

© Carson-Dellosa • CD-104909

Ecosystems

air | butterfly | fern | fish | rocks | soil | water | willow

the sun

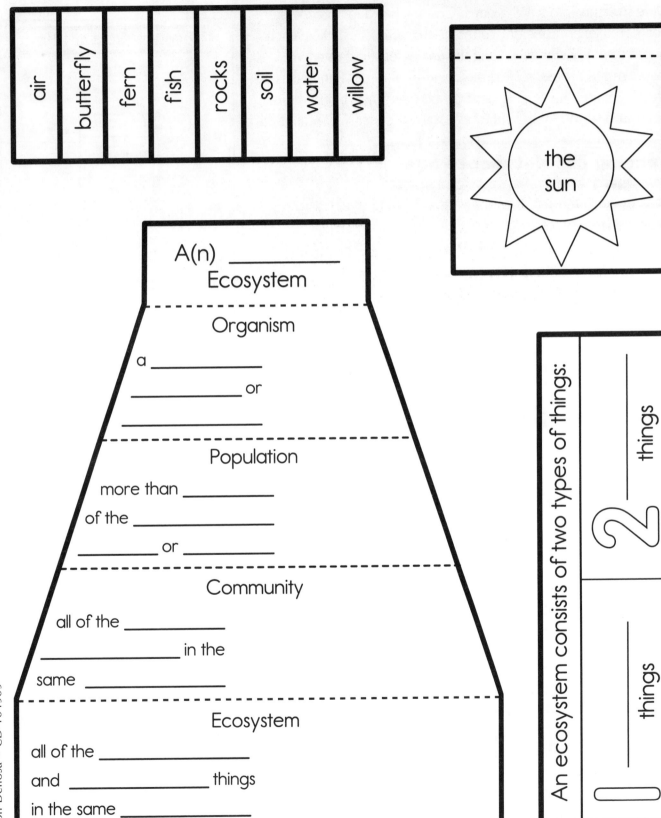

A(n) _____
Ecosystem

Organism

a _____

_____ or

_____

Population

more than _____

of the _____

_____ or _____

Community

all of the _____

_____ in the

same _____

Ecosystem

all of the _____

and _____ things

in the same _____

An ecosystem consists of two types of things:

2

_____ things

_____ things

⬭

Ecosystems: Oceans and Lakes

Introduction

Divide students into small groups. Give each group an ecosystem (ocean or lake) and one or two major characteristics. Have each group create a poster illustrating the characteristic(s) of each ecosystem. As a class, review the qualities of oceans and lakes. Focus on major characteristics (such as water type, temperature ranges, and surrounding landforms), animal life, and plant life.

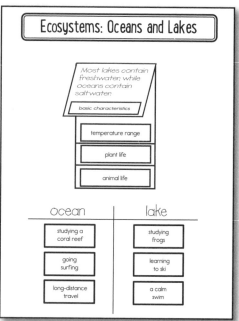

Creating the Notebook Page

Guide students through the following steps to complete the right-hand page in their notebooks.

1. Add a Table of Contents entry for the Ecosystems: Oceans and Lakes pages.

2. Cut out the title and glue it to the top of the page.

3. Cut out the two rectangular pieces on the solid lines. Fold each rectangle on the dashed lines. Fold the piece with the gray glue section so that it is inside the fold. Apply glue to the gray glue section and place the other folded rectangle on top so that the folds are nested and create a book with four cascading flaps. Make sure that the inside pages are facing up so that the edges of both pages are visible. Glue the flip book below the title.

4. Cut out the four qualities labels. Glue one label along the bottom edge of each flap (from top to bottom: *basic characteristics, temperature range, plant life, animal life*).

5. On the top flap, write a statement to compare an important basic characteristic of a lake with one of an ocean. On the second flap, write a statement to compare the potential temperature range of a lake with that of an ocean. On the third flap, write a statement to compare the plant life in a lake with that of an ocean. On the last flap, write a statement to compare the animals found in a lake with those in an ocean.

6. Draw a T-chart at the bottom of the page. Label the sides *ocean* and *lake*.

7. Cut out the six activity pieces and glue them in the correct columns on the T-chart.

Reflect on Learning

To complete the left-hand page, have students explain whether they would rather visit a lake or an ocean, using facts about each ecosystem to explain their preferences.

Ecosystems: Oceans and Lakes

basic characteristics

temperature range

plant life

animal life

a calm swim	going surfing
long-distance travel	learning to ski
studying a coral reef	studying frogs

glue

Ecosystems: Forests and Grasslands

Introduction

Have students draw items they associate with the words *grassland* and *forest*. Students should include plants and animals in their drawings. Ask students to share their drawings and confirm correct answers, explaining incorrect ones. For example, a picture of the grasslands likely would not have trees because there is not enough rainfall or nutrients in the soil to support trees, but a zebra or antelope would be correct. However, a zebra or antelope would struggle to navigate a forest environment populated by trees.

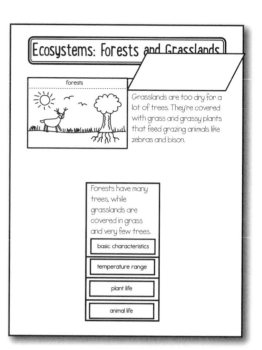

Creating the Notebook Page

Guide students through the following steps to complete the right-hand page in their notebooks.

1. Add a Table of Contents entry for the Ecosystems: Forests and Grasslands pages.

2. Cut out the title and glue it to the top of the page.

3. Cut out the flap book. Cut on the solid line to create two flaps. Apply glue to the back of the top section and attach it below the title. Draw an example of each ecosystem on the flap. Then, write information about each ecosystem under the appropriate flap.

4. Cut out the two rectangular pieces on the solid lines. Fold each rectangle on the dashed lines. Fold the piece with the gray glue section so that it is inside the fold. Apply glue to the gray glue section and place the other folded rectangle on top so that the folds are nested and create a book with four cascading flaps. Make sure that the inside pages are facing up so that the edges of both pages are visible. Glue the flip book below the title.

5. Cut out the four labels. Glue one label along the bottom edge of each flap (from top to bottom: *basic characteristic, temperature range, plant life, animal life*).

6. On the top flap, write a statement to compare an important basic characteristic of a forest with one of a grassland. On the second flap, write a statement to compare the potential temperature range of a forest with that of a grassland. On the third flap, write a statement to compare the plant life of a forest with that of a grassland. On the last flap, write a statement to compare the animals found in a forest with those found in a grassland.

Reflect on Learning

To complete the left-hand page, have students write a story with a character (person or animal) who moves from the forest to the grassland (or vice versa). Have students describe how the character must adapt to the new habitat by overcoming the challenges of the new environment.

Ecosystems: Forests and Grasslands

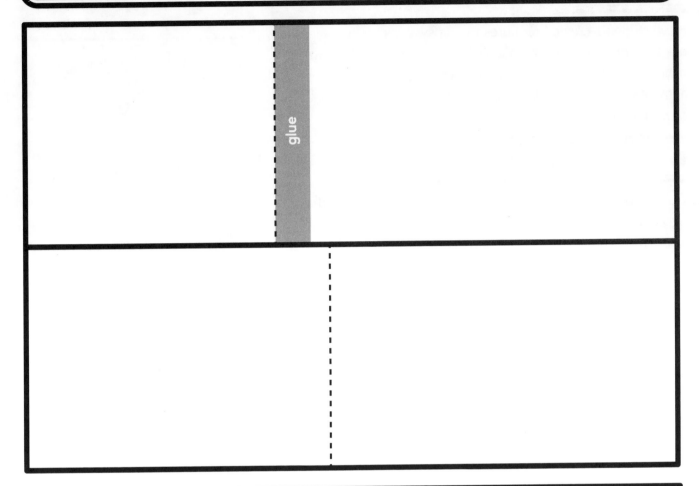

glue

forests   grasslands

basic characteristics	temperature range
plant life	animal life

Ecosystems Review

Introduction

Have students create brochures for ecosystems that the class has previously discussed. In addition to illustrating the covers, have students list details about the ecosystem in sections: special activities, animal life, plant life, and advice on how to dress, pack, or prepare for a visit.

Creating the Notebook Page

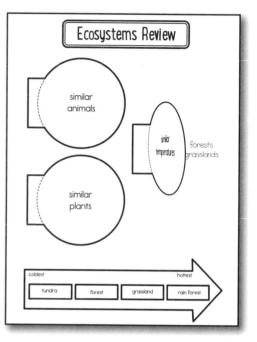

Guide students through the following steps to complete the right-hand page in their notebooks.

1. Add a Table of Contents entry for the Ecosystems Review pages.

2. Cut out the title and glue it to the top of the page.

3. Cut out the flaps. Apply glue to the back of the left sections and attach them to the page.

4. Under each flap, write at least two ecosystems that share the quality shown.

5. Cut out the arrow and glue it to the page below the flaps.

6. Cut out the names of the four ecosystems and glue them on the arrow in order, from coldest to hottest.

Reflect on Learning

To complete the left-hand page, have students write which ecosystem their favorite animal lives in. Students should support their opinions with details of how the plants, temperature, and basic characteristics of that ecosystem support the animal.

Answer Key
Similar temperatures: forest and grassland; Similar plants: forest and rainforest; Similar animals: ocean and lake; coldest to hottest: tundra, forest, grassland, rainforest

Ecosystems Review

similar
temperatures

similar
plants

similar
animals

coldest   hottest

| forest | rain forest | tundra | grassland |

Making Energy

Introduction

Have students list their meals from the past week. Have them name the categories of foods people eat (such as meats, fruits, vegetables, and grains). Ask students what they think plants eat. Discuss how it is possible that life can be sustained by such different sources of energy.

Creating the Notebook Page

Guide students through the following steps to complete the right-hand page in their notebooks.

1. Add a Table of Contents entry for the Making Energy pages.

2. Cut out the title and glue it to the top of the page.

3. Cut out the *All living things* flap book. Cut on the solid line to create two flaps. Apply glue to the back of the top section and attach it to the page below the title.

4. Complete the explanation. (All living things need **energy** to survive.) Discuss how plants and animals differ in how they get their energy. Under each flap, write the main source of energy for each type of organism.

5. Cut out the *photosynthesis* flap. Apply glue to the back of the left section and attach it pointing downward from the *plants* flap.

6. Under the flap, describe the process of photosynthesis and how it relates to plants and energy.

7. Cut out the flower and glue it to the bottom of the page.

8. Cut out the five arrows and the *chlorophyll* flap.

9. Glue the arrows around the flower to demonstrate the process of photosynthesis. Glue carbon dioxide and sunlight entering the flower on the left, and water entering from the roots. Glue oxygen and energy for animals leaving the flower on the right. Apply glue to the back of the left section of the chlorophyll flap and attach it near the leaf. Under the flap, describe the role chlorophyll plays in photosynthesis.

Reflect on Learning

To complete the left-hand page, have students consider why the balance between plants and animals is so important. What would happen if all of one or the other were gone?

Making Energy

All living things need _____ to survive.
Different organisms use different kinds of energy.

Plants	Animals

photosynthesis

carbon dioxide

water

sunlight

oxygen

* energy for animals

chlorophyll

Roles of Organisms

Introduction

Have students write about the process of getting, eating, and cleaning up lunch. Make sure they think about where the food comes from in addition to how it gets on their trays. Then, have students label steps to show when food is made, when food is eaten, and when food is cleaned up. Explain that these roles are also fulfilled in all ecosystems: producers (plants) create food sources, consumers take the food sources by eating the plants or eating the animals that fed on the plants, and decomposers help break down what is left behind.

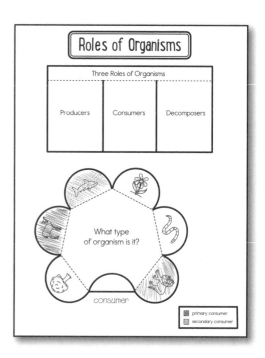

Creating the Notebook Page

Guide students through the following steps to complete the right-hand page in their notebooks.

1. Add a Table of Contents entry for the Roles of Organisms pages.

2. Cut out the title and glue it to the top of the page.

3. Cut out the *Three Roles of Organisms* flap book. Cut on the solid lines to create three flaps. Apply glue to the back of the top section and attach it to the page below the title.

4. Write the definitions of producers, consumers, and decomposers under each flap.

5. Cut out the petal flap book. Apply glue to the back of the center section and attach it to the page.

6. Under each flap, label each organism a producer, consumer, or decomposer.

7. Cut out the *primary consumer/secondary consumer* key. Glue it to the bottom of the page.

8. Color the boxes on the key two different colors. Then, color the petals to show which are primary consumers and which are secondary consumers.

Reflect on Learning

To complete the left-hand page, have students think about how extinction can affect an ecosystem. Ask them which would spoil an ecosystem most quickly: extinction of producers, consumers, or decomposers? Students should explain their answers.

Answer Key
flower: producer; worm: decomposer; lion: consumer; bird: consumer; tree: producer; deer: consumer; shark: consumer; primary consumer: deer; secondary consumers: lion, bird, shark

Roles of Organisms

Three Roles of Organisms		
Producers	Consumers	Decomposers

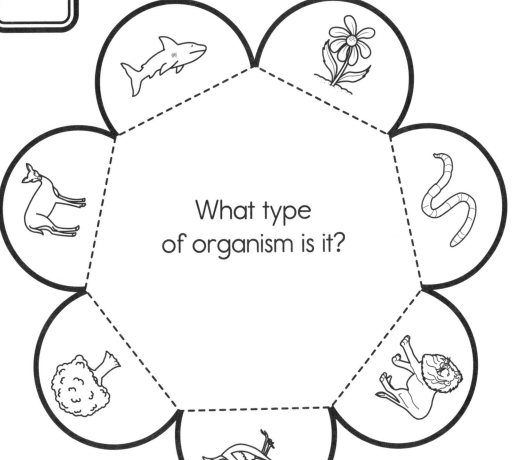

What type of organism is it?

☐ primary consumer
☐ secondary consumer

Food Chains

Introduction

Have students make a list of what they like to eat. As a class, discuss where each food comes from. How does each food get the nutrients and energy it passes on to us?

Creating the Notebook Page

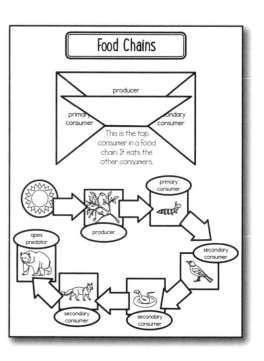

Guide students through the following steps to complete the right-hand page in their notebooks.

1. Add a Table of Contents entry for the Food Chains pages.

2. Cut out the title and glue it to the top of the page.

3. Cut out the *Vocabulary* flap book. Cut on the solid lines to create four flaps. Apply glue to the back of the center section and attach it below the title.

4. Write the definition of each term under the flap.

5. Cut out the picture and word pieces. (Note: You may want to position all pieces before gluing.) Glue them in the order that they are consumed, starting with the sun. Glue the correct label (*producer, primary consumer, secondary consumer,* or *apex predator*) next to each picture.

6. Cut out the arrows. Glue them to the page to show the flow of energy through the food chain. Then, brainstorm what would happen if you added a new animal to the food chain, such as an owl or a mouse. Introduce the idea of food webs. If desired, allow students to draw new animals and arrows to create a food web.

Reflect on Learning

To complete the left-hand page, have students research an ecosystem and show how at least five of its plants and animals are connected in a food chain. Students should make sure that at least one link is a producer and at least one link is an apex predator.

Food Chains

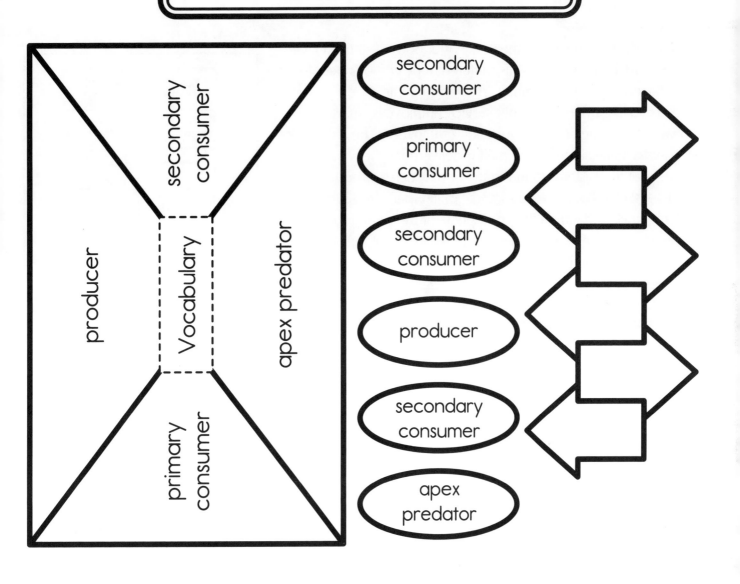

secondary consumer

primary consumer

secondary consumer

producer

secondary consumer

apex predator

producer

Vocabulary

secondary consumer

primary consumer

apex predator

Muscles and Movement

Introduction

Use this lesson to introduce the concept of body systems. Have students break into groups to list different types of jobs people might have in the same company. For example, in a post office, there are mail carriers, customer service employees, supervisors, and various sorting and transportation employees. They all work together to make sure that the mail is delivered. Give a brief overview of the systems found in the body (such as endocrine, digestive, skeletal, and nervous) and explain that some systems work together to handle different aspects of the same job, just like people in a company all handle different aspects of the work to accomplish the company's goals.

Creating the Notebook Page

Guide students through the following steps to complete the right-hand page in their notebooks.

1. Add a Table of Contents entry for the Muscles and Movement pages.

2. Cut out the title and glue it to the top of the page.

3. Cut out the puzzle pieces and the names of the systems.

4. Glue the appropriate label onto each puzzle piece.

5. Glue the puzzle pieces onto the page to create a four-piece puzzle.

6. Cut out the arrow and glue it below the puzzle.

7. Write a sentence on the arrow to describe how these systems work together. (For example, *The skeletal system supports the entire body, the muscular system moves it, the cardiovascular system supplies oxygen and nutrients, and the nervous system is in charge.*)

Reflect on Learning

To complete the left-hand page, have students write a paragraph from the perspective of particular bones or muscles, describing what they do and how they feel about it.

Answer Key
moves bones: muscular system; framework for the body: skeletal system; heart muscles: cardiovascular system; sends commands from brain: nervous system

Muscles and Movement

moves bones	framework for the body
muscular system	skeletal system
heart muscles	sends commands from the brain
cardiovascular system	nervous system

The skeletal system supports the entire body, the muscular system moves it, the cardiovascular system supplies oxygen, and the nervous system is in charge.

Muscles and Movement

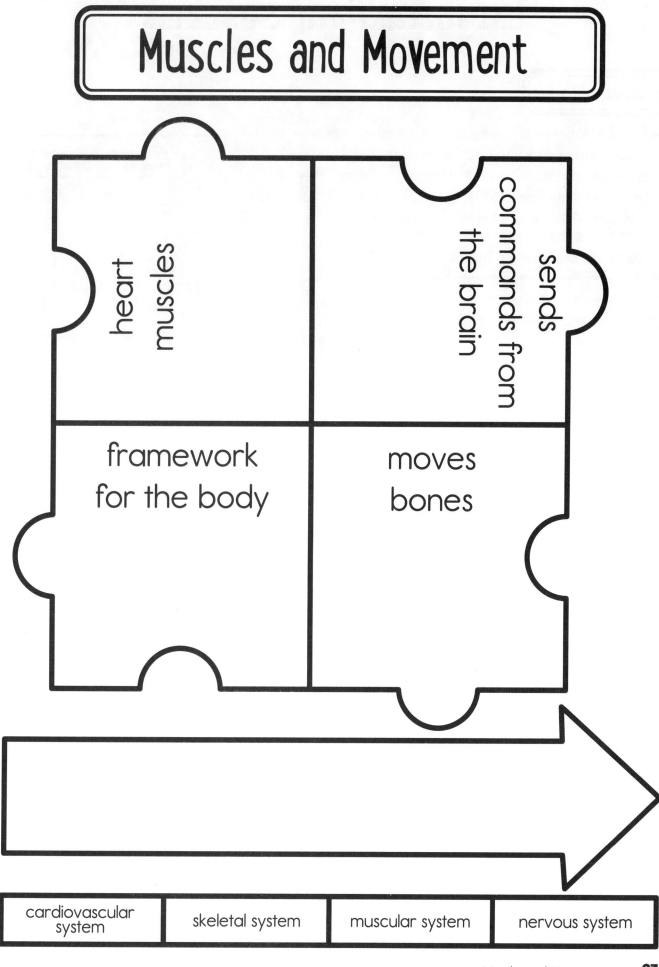

heart muscles

sends commands from the brain

framework for the body

moves bones

| cardiovascular system | skeletal system | muscular system | nervous system |

Essential Body Systems

Introduction

Review how multiple systems can work together to achieve similar goals. Ask students what three things humans need to survive. Write the answer (water, food, and air) on the board. Then, ask students to identify how their bodies interact with each essential item. Which system is needed for each one?

Creating the Notebook Page

Guide students through the following steps to complete the right-hand page in their notebooks.

1. Add a Table of Contents entry for the Essential Body Systems pages.

2. Cut out the title and glue it to the top of the page.

3. Cut out the puzzle pieces. Apply glue to the back of the left or right section of each puzzle piece and attach them to the page to create a three-piece flap puzzle.

4. Under each flap, describe the function of each system.

5. Cut out the pictures of the organs and glue them on the matching system puzzle pieces. You may choose to draw lines on the circulatory system piece to symbolize the veins and arteries as well.

6. Cut out the arrow and glue it below the puzzle.

7. Write a sentence on the arrow to describe how these systems are essential to the human body.

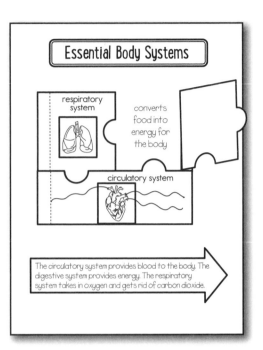

Reflect on Learning

To complete the left-hand page, have students explain which, if any, of these systems could be deemed more important than the others. Answers should include specific details about how these systems impact the rest of the body.

Comparing Systems

function of the nervous system	function of the circulatory system

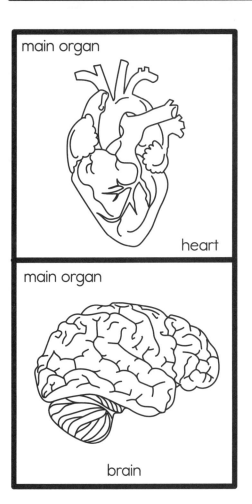

main organ

heart

main organ

brain

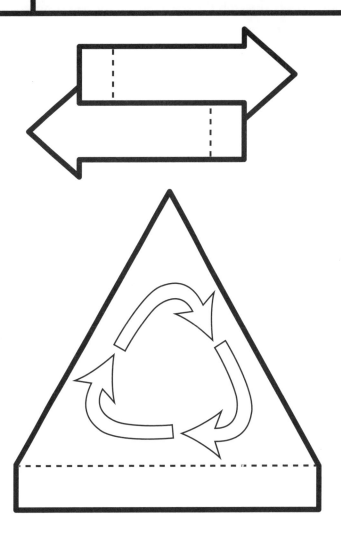

Nervous System

Circulatory System

Inherited Traits

Introduction

Have students look at images of different types of "parents"—human, animal, and plant—and have them predict what the offspring will look like. Have students explain their answers. For example, why might they have predicted that two blond parents would have a blond child or that a red flower and a white flower might create a pink flower?

Creating the Notebook Page

Guide students through the following steps to complete the right-hand page in their notebooks.

1. Add a Table of Contents entry for the Inherited Traits pages.

2. Cut out the title and glue it to the top of the page.

3. Cut out the *Inherited Traits/Learned Traits* flap book. Cut on the solid line to create two flaps. Apply glue to the back of the top section and attach it below the title.

4. Write the definition of each term under the flap. Draw a vertical line below the flaps to create a T-chart with the *Inherited Traits* and *Learned Traits* flaps as the headers.

5. Cut out the traits and glue them in the appropriate columns of the T-chart.

6. Cut out the *My Inherited Traits/My Learned Traits* flap book. Cut on the solid line to create two flaps. Apply glue to the back of the top section and attach it below the T-chart.

7. Write some of your own inherited or learned traits under the appropriate flaps.

Reflect on Learning

To complete the left-hand page, have students write about a learned trait they admire in someone else. Have students include how they could try to develop this trait. For example, if they admire someone else's handwriting, they could practice their own. If they admire someone else's hard work, they could set goals and practice working toward them. Students should also write about whether they think inherited traits can be changed. Why or why not?

Inherited Traits

Inherited Traits	Acquired ~~Learned~~ Traits 

color blindness	hair color
eye color	handwriting
diet	height
favorite food	language

My Inherited Traits	My Learned Traits

Matter

Introduction

Have students debate about what the smallest thing on Earth is. If a student gives the answer "atom," have her explain what an atom is. If no student gives that answer, introduce the idea of an atom to the class, telling students that atoms can vary in structure (which creates different elements) but are the smallest complete part of any element or chemical compound. Explain that atoms are so small that they cannot be seen without using special microscopes.

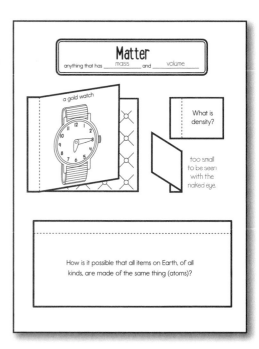

Creating the Notebook Page

Guide students through the following steps to complete the right-hand page in their notebooks.

1. Add a Table of Contents entry for the Matter pages.

2. Cut out the title and glue it to the top of the page.

3. Complete the definition of *matter* (anything that has **mass** and **volume**).

4. Cut out the two large flaps. Apply glue to the gray glue section of the *atoms of gold* flap. Place the gold watch flap on top to create a stacked two-flap book. Apply glue to the back of the left section and attach the flap book to the left side of the page.

5. Under the bottom flap, describe the arrangement of atoms in a substance. (Atoms always arrange themselves in an organized way.)

6. Cut out the two small flaps. Apply glue to the back of the left sections and attach them to the right of the *a gold watch* flap book.

7. Define density under the *What is . . .* flap (the amount of matter in an object). Complete the sentence under the *Atoms are . . .* flap. (Atoms are **too small to be seen with the naked eye**.)

8. Cut out the long flap. Apply glue to the back of the top section and attach it to the bottom of the page.

9. Discuss how everything in the world is made of atoms, but most things look and behave differently. For example, solids and liquids are both made of atoms but behave very differently. Answer the question under the flap. (There are different types of atoms and they can combine in many different ways.)

Reflect on Learning

To complete the left-hand page, have students make a T-chart and label the columns *matter* and *not matter*. Students should write at least three items in each column.

Matter

anything that has _____ and _____

atoms of gold

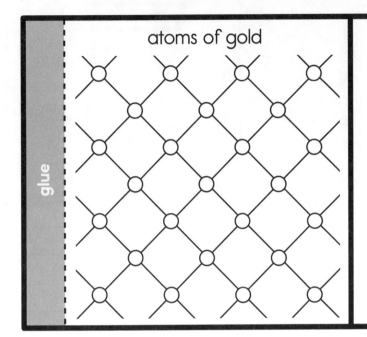

glue

a gold watch

What is density?

Atoms are . . .

How is it possible that all items on Earth, of all kinds, are made of the same thing (atoms)?

States of Matter

Introduction

Have students write a story about a person who can change his appearance back and forth. Stories should explain how the change is triggered. Allow students to share their stories and have them create categories to show how they changed their characters. For example, how many drank a special potion, got angry, changed at will, or pushed a button? Point out that most forms of matter can change states without becoming a different substance, and that most of the time, that change is triggered by the addition or removal of heat.

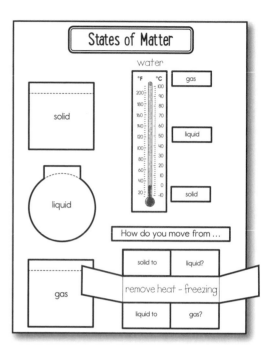

Creating the Notebook Page

Guide students through the following steps to complete the right-hand page in their notebooks.

1. Add a Table of Contents entry for the States of Matter pages.

2. Cut out the title and glue it to the top of the page.

3. Cut out the *solid, liquid*, and *gas* flaps. Apply glue to the back of the top sections and attach them to the page in a column on the left side.

4. Describe each state of matter under the appropriate flap.

5. Cut out the thermometer and the *solid, liquid*, and *gas* labels. Glue the thermometer to the right of the top two flaps.

6. Label the thermometer *water* and color segments with three different shades to show the temperature ranges at which each state exists. Glue each label next to the thermometer to show which state a temperature range represents.

7. Cut out the *How do you* piece. Glue it below the thermometer.

8. Cut out the shutter fold. Cut on the solid lines to create six flaps. Apply glue to the gray glue section and attach it below the *How do you* piece. Fold the flaps toward the center.

9. Under each flap, write whether heat needs to be added or removed to complete the phase change. Then, write the name of the state change.

Reflect on Learning

To complete the left-hand page, have students explain why it is valuable to know the freezing and melting points of various substances. What does this enable us to do?

States of Matter

solid	gas

liquid

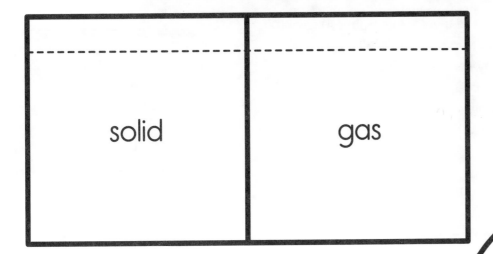

How do you move from ...		
solid	liquid	gas

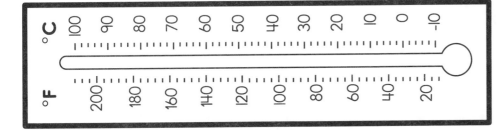

liquid?		solid to
solid?	glue	liquid to
gas?		liquid to

Physical and Chemical Changes

Introduction

Have students separate and label the ingredients from a bag of trail mix. Then, have students attempt to do the same with a slice of bread. Have students discuss why some things cannot be "un-mixed" while others can. Discuss that some changes we make to items go beyond physical changes. Sometimes, we actually change their chemical composition.

Caution: Before beginning any food activity, ask families' permission and inquire about students' food allergies and religious or other food restrictions.

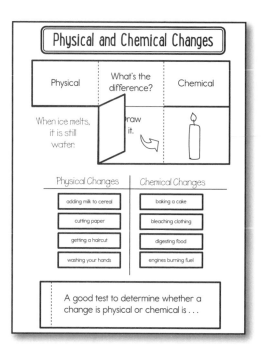

Creating the Notebook Page

Guide students through the following steps to complete the right-hand page in their notebooks.

1. Add a Table of Contents entry for the Physical and Chemical Changes pages.

2. Cut out the title and glue it to the top of the page.

3. Cut out the *What's the difference?* flap book. Cut on the solid lines to create four flaps. Apply glue to the back of the center section and attach it to the page below the title.

4. Write the definition for each type of change under the top flaps. On the bottom flaps, draw an example of each type of change. Under each bottom flap, describe how each drawing represents that type of change.

5. Below the flap book, draw a T-chart. Label the sides *physical changes* and *chemical changes*.

6. Cut out and glue the examples of changes in the correct column of the T-chart. If desired, add your own examples to each side.

7. Cut out the *A good test* flap. Apply glue to the back of the left edge and attach it to the bottom of the page.

8. Complete the sentence under the flap. (A good test to determine whether a change is physical or chemical is **to decide whether or not the change can be undone.**)

Reflect on Learning

To complete the left-hand page, have students describe one physical change and one chemical change that they have witnessed.

Physical and Chemical Changes

Physical	What's the difference?	Chemical
	Draw it.	

adding milk to cereal	digesting food
baking a cake	engines burning fuel
bleaching clothing	getting a haircut
cutting paper	washing your hands

A good test to determine whether a change is physical or chemical is . . .

Forces

Introduction

Demonstrate gravity by dropping an item from shoulder level. Ask students how they would keep the item from falling straight down. They may answer that someone could catch it, hit it, or put something between the item and the floor to make it bounce or deflect. Explain that all of these are examples of forces (gravity, as well as hitting or deflecting the item).

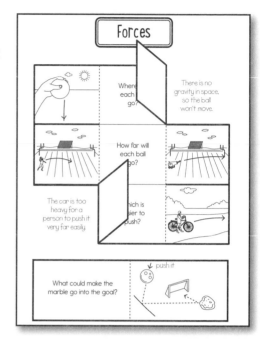

Creating the Notebook Page

Guide students through the following steps to complete the right-hand page in their notebooks.

1. Add a Table of Contents entry for the Forces pages.

2. Cut out the title and glue it to the top of the page.

3. Cut out the large flap book. Cut on the solid lines to create six flaps. Apply glue to the back of the center section and attach it below the title.

4. On the top flaps, draw arrows to show where the ball will go. Under the top flaps, write what will happen to the ball if dropped in each situation and why. Discuss how gravity or the absence of gravity affects the ball in each picture.

5. On the center flaps, draw a line to show the approximate distance each ball will go. Under the center flaps, write how far each ball will travel in each situation and why. Discuss how force affects the distance in each situation.

6. On the bottom flaps, draw a line to show how far each vehicle would move in the same amount of time. Under the bottom flaps, write how far each vehicle will move given the same amount of force in each situation and why. Discuss how mass can change the effect when the same amount of force is used.

7. Cut out the *What could make* flap. Apply glue to the back of the left section and attach it to the bottom of the page.

8. On the flap, draw objects or another force (such as wind) to help change the direction of the marble after it has been set in motion. Under the flap, explain how forces are related to changes in direction.

Reflect on Learning

To complete the left-hand page, have students write a paragraph to describe a force other than gravity (such as wind) and how it can act on objects.

Forces

Where will each ball go?

How far will each ball go?

Which is easier to push?

What could make the marble go into the goal?

Forms of Energy

Introduction

Have students inventory the energy being used in the classroom at that moment. What things are drawing electricity? Is anything using another type of fuel? What is the source of the light energy the class is using?

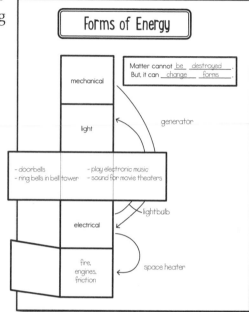

Creating the Notebook Page

Guide students through the following steps to complete the right-hand page in their notebooks.

1. Add a Table of Contents entry for the Forms of Energy pages.

2. Cut out the title and glue it to the top of the page.

3. Cut out the flap book. Cut on the solid lines to create 10 flaps. Apply glue to the gray glue section and attach it to the left side of the page. Fold the flaps toward the center to form mini brochures with the words on top.

4. On the right-hand flap of each mini brochure, write at least one source of that type of energy. With the brochure fully open, write applications of that type of energy.

5. Cut out the *Matter cannot* piece. Glue it to the top of the right side of the page.

6. Complete the explanation. (Matter cannot **be destroyed**. But, it can **change forms**.)

7. Draw an arrow from one form of energy to another to the right of the flap book. Label each arrow with an example of that type of transformation. For example, an arrow drawn from electrical to sound could be labeled with *electric speakers*.

Reflect on Learning

To complete the left-hand page, have students explain how they will use at least three of the types of energy explored in the lesson in the near future.

Forms of Energy

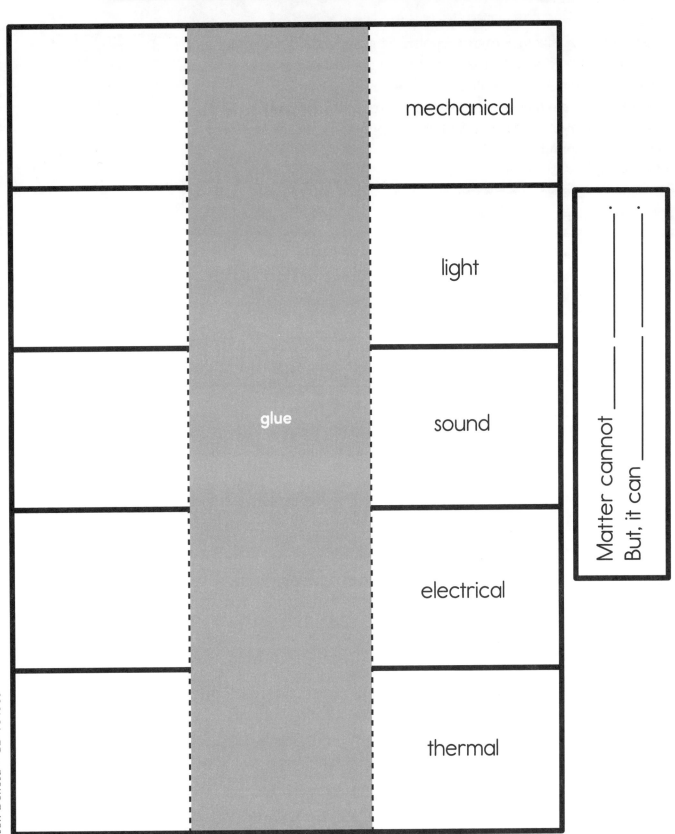

mechanical

light

glue

sound

electrical

thermal

Matter cannot _____
But, it can _____

Light and Sound

Introduction

Have students use overhead lights, flashlights, or the sun to demonstrate ways that they can manipulate light, such as blocking it with their hands, casting shadows, or reflecting off of some surfaces. Then, have students attempt to keep others around them from hearing a message or communicating with someone across the playground. Point out what they are doing physically to manipulate the sound, such as leaning in close, cupping hands, or turning away from or toward certain people.

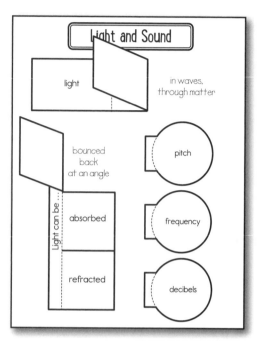

Creating the Notebook Page

Guide students through the following steps to complete the right-hand page in their notebooks.

1. Add a Table of Contents entry for the Light and Sound pages.

2. Cut out the title and glue it to the top of the page.

3. Cut out the *How do they travel?* flap book. Apply glue to the back of the center section and attach it below the title.

4. Write how each form of energy travels under the correct flap. Discuss how light travels in a straight line and does not need to travel through matter, and how sound travels in waves and must travel through matter.

5. Cut out the *Light can be . . .* flap book. Cut on the solid lines to create three flaps. Apply glue to the back of the left section and attach it to the left side of the page.

6. Under each flap, write a definition for the word.

7. Cut out the *pitch, frequency,* and *decibels* flaps. Apply glue to the back of the left sections and attach them to the right side of the page.

8. Write a definition for the word under each flap.

Reflect on Learning

To complete the left-hand page, have students explain why some of the actions they took to manipulate light and sound in the introduction were effective. What property of light allows it to be blocked by your body? Why does cupping your hand around your mouth or turning your body change the way a sound travels?

Light and Sound

light	How do they travel?	sound

Light can be...

reflected

absorbed

refracted

pitch

frequency

decibels

Types of Heat

Introduction

Have students write on self-stick notes about a way to warm up on a cold day. Have them share their ideas, such as using blankets, lighting a fire, drinking hot cocoa, etc. As a class, sort the self-stick notes by what type of heat they represent. Explain how some ways to warm up, such as using a heater, take heat from other sources; while others, such as rubbing hands together, create heat that was not previously there.

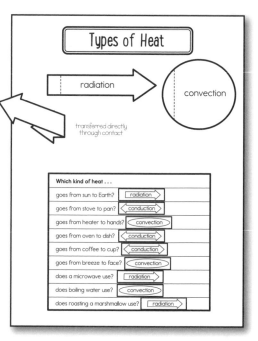

Creating the Notebook Page

Guide students through the following steps to complete the right-hand page in their notebooks.

1. Add a Table of Contents entry for the Types of Heat pages.

2. Cut out the title and glue it to the top of the page.

3. Cut out the *conduction*, *convection*, and *radiation* flaps. Apply glue to the back of the left section of the flaps and attach them to the page below the title.

4. Under each flap, explain how that type of heat is transferred (conduction: heat is transferred directly through contact; convection: heat is transferred indirectly through air or water; radiation: heat is given off in waves).

5. Cut out the *What kind of heat* piece and glue it to the bottom of the page.

6. Cut out the *conduction*, *convection*, and *radiation* labels. Glue the appropriate label next to each question.

Reflect on Learning

To complete the left-hand page, have students explain why one heating technique is not necessarily effective for all materials. What would happen if we could only use one type of heat?

Answer Key
From top to bottom: radiation; conduction; convection; conduction; conduction; convection; radiation; convection; radiation

Types of Heat

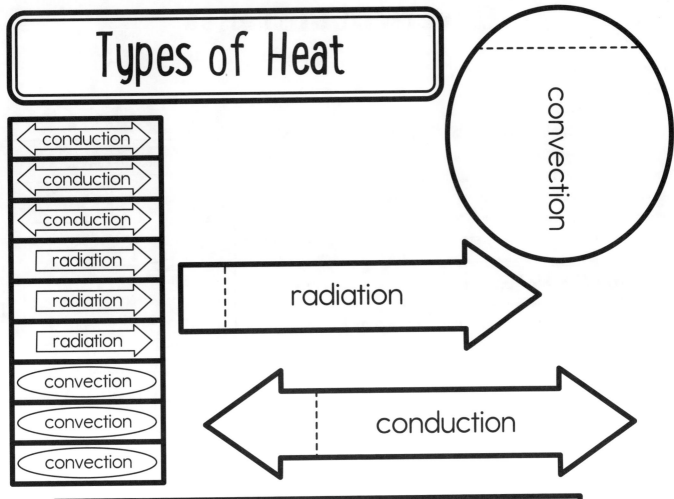

conduction
conduction
conduction
radiation
radiation
radiation
convection
convection
convection

convection

radiation

conduction

Which kind of heat . . .
goes from sun to Earth?
goes from stove to pan?
goes from heater to hands?
goes from oven to dish?
goes from coffee to cup?
goes from breeze to face?
does a microwave use?
does boiling water use?
does roasting a marshmallow use?

Electrical Currents

Introduction

Have students examine an electrical plug, an outlet cover, and an outlet (from a distance). Have students write what they notice about the plugs and outlets, in an attempt to obtain meaning from their observations. For instance, why is it safe to touch the plastic childproof outlet cover but not to touch the metal prongs of the plug while plugging it in? Why are there two prongs on the plug?

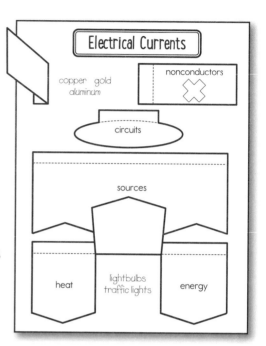

Creating the Notebook Page

Guide students through the following steps to complete the right-hand page in their notebooks.

1. Add a Table of Contents entry for the Electrical Currents pages.

2. Cut out the title and glue it to the top of the page.

3. Cut out the *conductors* and *nonconductors* flaps. Apply glue to the back of the left sections and attach them side by side below the title.

4. Write examples of conductors and nonconductors under each flap.

5. Cut out the *circuits* flap. Apply glue to the back of the top section and attach it below the *conductors/nonconductors* flaps.

6. Write the key factor of functional electrical circuits under the *circuits* flap (all circuits must be a closed loop).

7. Cut out the *sources* flap. Apply glue to the back of the top section and attach it below the *circuits* flap.

8. Write several examples of sources of electricity under the *sources* flap (batteries, generators, the power company, etc.).

9. Cut out the *outputs* flap book. Cut on the solid lines to create three flaps. Apply glue to the back of the top section and attach it to the bottom of the page.

10. Write a use for each type of electrical output under the flaps.

Reflect on Learning

To complete the left-hand page, have students revisit the details they observed in the introduction. Why does the plastic cover make the outlet safe? Why does the plug have two prongs? Which other details were significant?

Essential Body Systems

respiratory
system

digestive
system

circulatory system

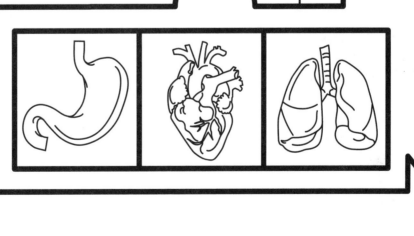

Digestive System

Introduction

Have students explain why nutrients from food can't be absorbed through skin or by smell. Why must we eat food to get its nutrients? Then, point out that people do not have broccoli running through their veins. We need our digestive systems to transform nutrients from the food form into forms our cells can use.

Creating the Notebook Page

Guide students through the following steps to complete the right-hand page in their notebooks.

1. Add a Table of Contents entry for the Digestive System pages.

2. Cut out the title and glue it to the top of the page.

3. Cut out the diagram of the digestive system and glue it below the title.

4. Cut out the six flaps. Apply glue to the back of the top sections and attach them to the appropriate places on the diagram. Draw lines to connect the labels to the correct part.

5. Under each organ or body part flap, write its purpose during digestion.

6. Write a short paragraph at the bottom of the page to explain the digestive system's purpose and how it works.

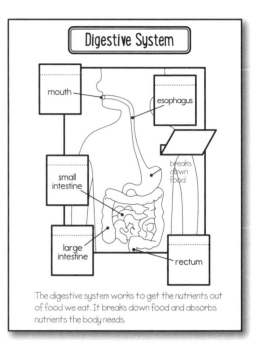

The digestive system works to get the nutrients out of food we eat. It breaks down food and absorbs nutrients the body needs.

Reflect on Learning

To complete the left-hand page, have students describe a machine that could help replace a digestive organ. What tasks would the machine need to perform? To what other organs would it need to connect?

Electrical Currents

conductors

nonconductors

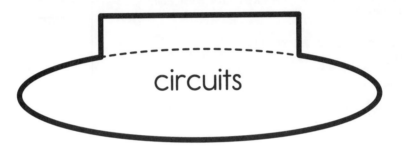

circuits

outputs

heat   light   energy

sources

The Water Cycle

Each student will need a brass paper fastener to complete this page.

Introduction

Show students a globe or an image of Earth from space. Ask them which they think is bigger: all of the oceans on Earth or all of the land. Tell them that the oceans comprise over 70 percent of Earth's surface and have them list places where water is found in nature (streams, rivers, oceans, lakes, and ponds). Explain that the water cycle is vital to water's distribution across Earth and our ability to survive.

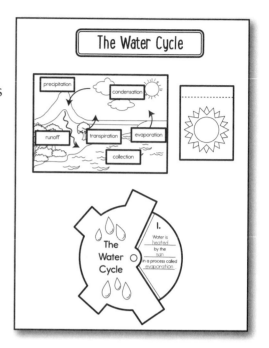

Creating the Notebook Page

Guide students through the following steps to complete the right-hand page in their notebooks.

1. Add a Table of Contents entry for *The Water Cycle* pages.

2. Cut out the title and glue it to the top of the page.

3. Cut out the diagram and glue it to the left side of the page below the title. Cut out the labels and glue them onto the diagram to label each part of the water cycle.

4. Cut out the sun flap. Apply glue to the back of the top section and attach it to the right of the diagram.

5. Under the flap, describe the importance of the sun in the water cycle.

6. Cut out the circular pieces. Place *The Water Cycle* piece on top of the circle with the steps of the cycle. Push a brass paper fastener through the center dots of the circles to attach them. It may be helpful to create the hole in each piece separately first. Apply glue to the back of the *Water Cycle* piece tabs and attach it to the bottom of the page. The brass paper fastener should not go through the page, and the step-by-step circle should spin freely.

7. Fill in the blanks on the circle to describe the steps of the water cycle. (1. Water is **heated** by the **sun** in a process called **evaporation**. 2. Water **cools** and the droplets form **clouds** in a process called **condensation**. 3. Water droplets **fall** as **precipitation**.)

Reflect on Learning

To complete the left-hand page, have students imagine what would happen if the water cycle did not exist. How would water travel inland from the oceans? How would populations living inland be affected?

The Water Cycle

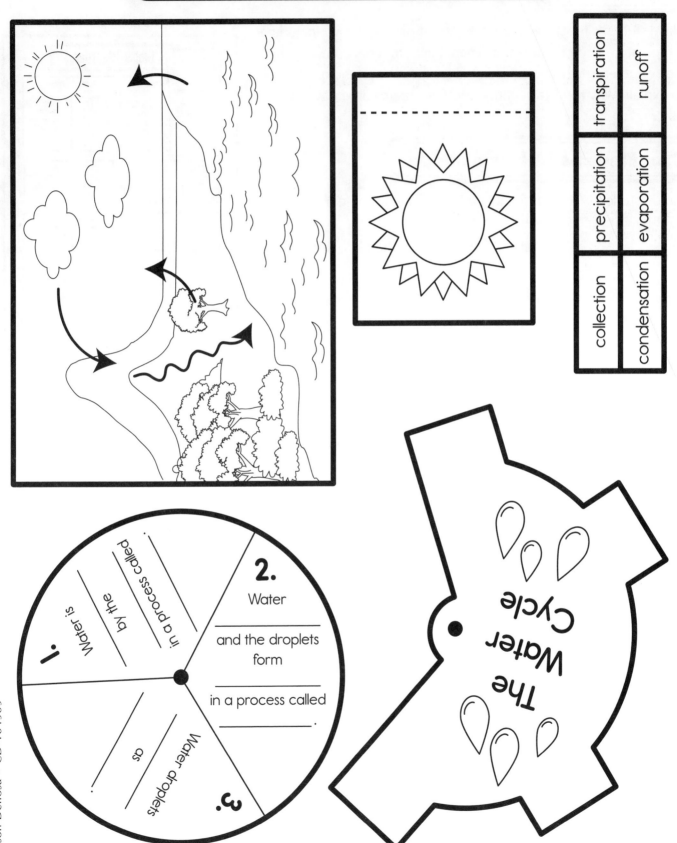

transpiration

runoff

precipitation

evaporation

collection

condensation

1. Water is _____ by the _____ in a process called _____.

2. Water _____ and the droplets form _____ in a process called _____.

3. Water droplets _____ as _____.

The Water Cycle

Global Weather

Introduction

Have students record weather for several days in a row, including temperature and precipitation. Then, have students compare the real weather to what was predicted for those days and ask them to explain why reports might be more accurate some days than others.

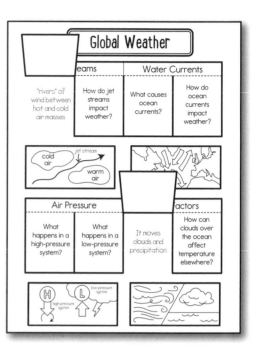

Creating the Notebook Page

Guide students through the following steps to complete the right-hand page in their notebooks.

1. Add a Table of Contents entry for the Global Weather pages.

2. Cut out the title and glue it to the top of the page.

3. Cut out the *Jet Streams/Water Currents* flap book. Cut on the solid lines to create four flaps. Apply glue to the back of the top section and attach it below the title.

4. Answer the questions under the flaps.

5. Cut out the *Air Pressure/Other Factors* flap book. Cut on the solid lines to create four flaps. Apply glue to the back of the top section and attach it below the other flap book, leaving several lines of space between the two rows of flap books.

6. Answer the questions under the flaps.

7. Cut out the diagrams and glue them below the correct sides of the flap book.

8. Label the diagrams with the appropriate terms (jet stream, water currents, high-pressure system, low-pressure system).

Reflect on Learning

To complete the left-hand page, have students look at the weather recorded in the introduction. Have them describe the types of changes that could have caused the weather they experienced.

Global Weather

Other Factors		Air Pressure	
How can clouds over the ocean affect temperature elsewhere?	How does the wind affect weather?	What happens in a low-pressure system?	What happens in a high-pressure system?

Jet Streams		Water Currents	
What are jet streams?	How do jet streams impact weather?	What causes ocean currents?	How do ocean currents impact weather?

Weather vs. Climate

Have students describe today's weather and the weather of another recent day that was notably different. Ask students which day was most indicative of the season in the area. For example, if students are describing both a warm day and a cool day in the middle of summer, which one is most appropriate for the season?

Creating the Notebook Page

Guide students through the following steps to complete the right-hand page in their notebooks.

1. Add a Table of Contents entry for the Weather vs. Climate pages.

2. Cut out the title and glue it to the top of the page.

3. Cut out the *Define it!* flap book. Apply glue to the back of the center section and attach it to the page below the title.

4. Write the definition of each term under the flap. (Weather is the current condition of the air and atmosphere in a given time and place. Climate is the average weather conditions for a time and place.)

5. Draw a T-chart below the flap book. Cut out the *weather* and *climate* labels to title the T-chart.

6. Cut out the examples and glue them in the appropriate columns.

7. Cut out the *Major World Climate Zones* map. Glue it to the bottom of the page.

8. Color each box on the key a different color. Color each region of the map according to the key to differentiate the world climate zones. (Above 60°N and below 60°S are the polar zones. From 30°N to 60°N and 30°S to 60°S are the temperate zones. From 30°S to 30°N is the tropical zone.)

Reflect on Learning

To complete the left-hand page, have students write a paragraph to describe their perceptions of the climate for their area. Is it hotter or colder than other parts of the planet? Is it typically dry or rainy? What precipitation or other weather conditions characterize the area?

Weather vs. Climate

weather	Define it!	climate

weather
climate

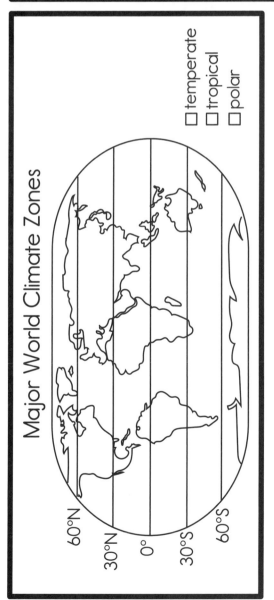

Major World Climate Zones

□ temperate
□ tropical
□ polar

60°N
30°N
0°
30°S
60°S

a hot summer day
an average of 30" of rainfall a year
based on current measurements
based on long-term data
It rained on Monday.
long-term time frame
short-term time frame
long, dry summers

Objects in the Solar System

Introduction

Have students review the parts of the solar system. Write the names of the planets on index cards. Give one card to each student and designate one wall of the classroom as the location of the sun. Challenge students with planet cards to place themselves in the correct order. For an added challenge, have students place themselves without talking. Then, as a class, discuss the many other types of objects in the solar system. Allow students to volunteer answers and record a list on the board.

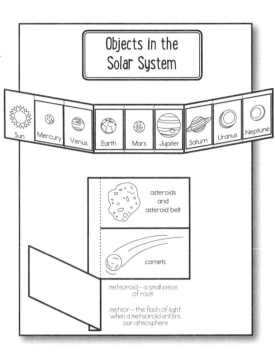

Creating the Notebook Page

Guide students through the following steps to complete the right-hand page in their notebooks.

1. Add a Table of Contents entry for the Objects in the Solar System pages.

2. Cut out the title and glue it to the top of the page.

3. Cut out the long piece with the sun at the end. Fold in the two outer sections on the dashed lines. Apply glue to the back of the center section and attach it below the title.

4. Write *The Sun and Planets* on the top flap. Cut out the planet pieces. Unfold the long piece and glue the planets in order.

5. Cut out the flap book. Cut on the solid lines to create three flaps. Apply glue to the back of the left section and attach it to the bottom of the page.

6. Under each flap, describe each object of the solar system.

Reflect on Learning

To complete the left-hand page, have students choose two objects in the solar system to compare and contrast in a Venn diagram.

	Venus
	Uranus
	Saturn
	Mercury
	Mars
	Neptune
	Jupiter
	Earth
	Sun

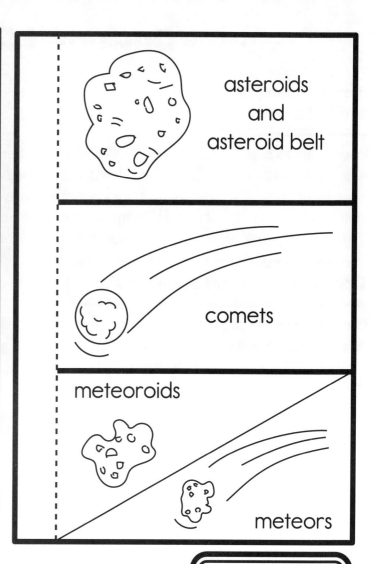

asteroids and asteroid belt

comets

meteoroids

meteors

Objects in the Solar System

Days and Seasons

Introduction

Have students read the Greek myth of Persephone. Then, discuss why the Greeks thought the seasons changed and discuss the purpose of myths. Explain that over time, scientists have been able to learn more about our planet and solar system. So, now we understand the true reason why seasons change.

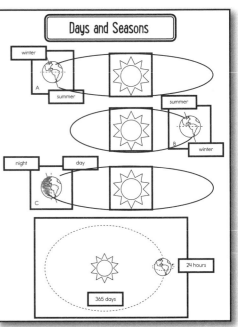

Creating the Notebook Page

Guide students through the following steps to complete the right-hand page in their notebooks.

1. Add a Table of Contents entry for the Days and Seasons pages.

2. Cut out the title and glue it to the top of the page.

3. Cut out the sun and Earth pieces. Glue the sun pieces in a column below the title. Glue *A* to the left of the sun piece in the first row. Glue *B* to the right of the sun piece in the second row. Place *C* on either side of the sun piece in the third row. After gluing down each Earth piece, draw an orbit for each Earth around its sun.

4. Cut out the *summer* and *winter* labels. Glue them on *A* and *B* to show which hemisphere is experiencing summer and which is experiencing winter.

5. Cut out the *night* and *day* labels. Glue them to show which side of Earth is experiencing night and which side is experiencing day on *C*. Shade the side of Earth that is experiencing night.

6. Cut out the diagram and glue it to the bottom of the page.

7. Cut out the *24 hours* and *365 days* labels and glue them to the appropriate orbit in the diagram.

Reflect on Learning

To complete the left-hand page, have students write a letter to the Greeks to explain the real origin of the seasons. How will students explain orbits and Earth's axis to people who have never heard of them before?

Days and Seasons

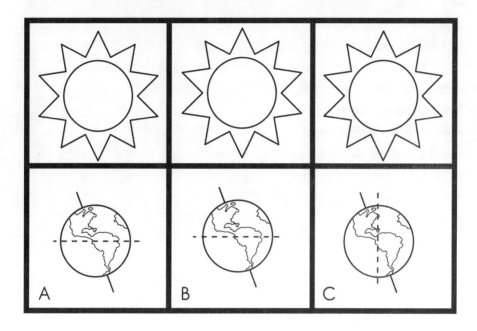

| 24 hours | 365 days | night | day | winter | winter | summer | summer |

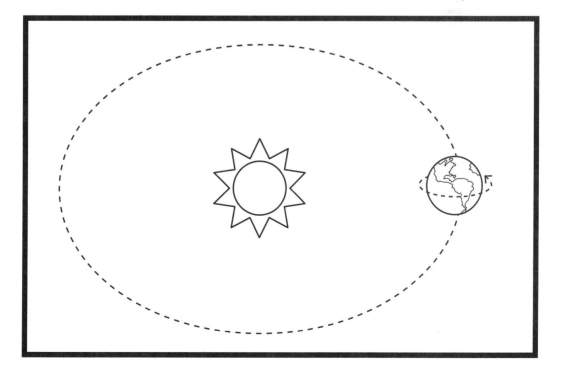

Days

Introduction

Have students write about a day that seemed especially long and a day that flew by quickly. Ask students what causes days to feel shorter or longer.

Creating the Notebook Page

Guide students through the following steps to complete the right-hand page in their notebooks.

1. Add a Table of Contents entry for the Days pages.

2. Cut out the title and glue it to the top of the page.

3. Cut out the graph flap. Apply glue to the back of the top section and attach it below the title. Make sure to leave room for the other flaps at the bottom of the page.

4. Cut out the chart showing sunrise and sunset times. Glue it under the graph flap.

5. For each row, use the chart to color the times that show when the sun was visible that day.

6. Cut out the flap book and flap. On the flap book, cut on the solid line to create two flaps. Apply glue to the back of each top section and attach them below the graph.

7. Use the graph to answer each question under the flap.

Reflect on Learning

To complete the left-hand page, have students explain why the longest days of the year are also typically the warmest.

Days

	12 am	1	2	3	4	5	6	7	8	9	10	11	12 pm	1	2	3	4	5	6	7	8	9	10	11
Jan. 5																								
Feb. 14																								
June 14																								
Aug. 2																								
Sept. 27																								
Nov. 6																								

Which season had the longest days?

Which season had the shortest days?

What day was the equinox in that year?

	Sunrise	Sunset
January 5	7:32	5:31
February 14	7:10	6:01
June 14	6:04	8:38
August 2	6:29	8:26
September 27	7:12	7:12
November 6	6:47	5:42

Soil Movement

Introduction

Have students describe the land surrounding where they live. Is there a creek? A hill? Have students be as thorough as possible. Guide students through drawing and labeling an aerial map. Discuss with them the types of landscape that are common in your area (mountains, bodies of water, etc.) and point out that most landforms are created by forces that move soil.

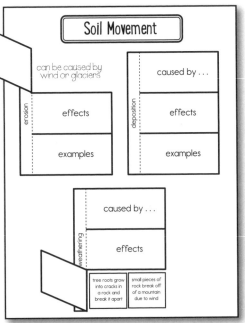

Creating the Notebook Page

Guide students through the following steps to complete the right-hand page in their notebooks.

1. Add a Table of Contents entry for the Soil Movement pages.

2. Cut out the title and glue it to the top of the page.

3. Cut out the *erosion, deposition,* and *weathering* flap books. Cut on the solid lines to create three flaps on each book. Apply glue to the back of the left sections and attach them to the page below the title.

4. Write the cause of each force under the *caused by . . .* flap and describe how that process affects the surrounding environment under the *effects* flap.

5. Cut out the six examples and glue them under the *examples* flap of the matching force.

Reflect on Learning

To complete the left-hand page, have students write about what could have formed one of the land characteristics they described in the introduction.

Soil Movement

deposition

caused by . . .

effects

examples

weathering

caused by . . .

effects

examples

erosion

caused by . . .

effects

examples

a river slowly wears its way down through the bedrock	small pieces of rock break off of a mountain due to wind
sand piles up as dunes	tree roots grow into cracks in a rock and break it apart
silt builds up at the mouth of a river	waves on a shoreline wash sand away

Rocks

Introduction

Have students write about where they might find rocks and minerals. See how many students included less obvious answers, like countertops (marble and granite), jewelry (diamonds, emeralds, and rubies), and sculptures (marble or soapstone). Ask them to describe one way people use rocks in everyday life.

Creating the Notebook Page

Guide students through the following steps to complete the right-hand page in their notebooks.

1. Add a Table of Contents entry for the Rocks pages.

2. Cut out the title and glue it to the top of the page.

3. Cut out the flap book. Cut on the solid lines to create six flaps. Apply glue to the back of the left section and attach it to the page below the title.

4. For each section of the flap book, describe how that type of rock is formed under the top flap and give examples of that type of rock under the bottom flap.

5. Cut out the diagram of the rock cycle and the labels. Glue the diagram to the bottom of the page. Glue the labels to the correct arrows to show how the rock cycle works.

Reflect on Learning

To complete the left-hand page, have students write an interview with a rock, asking it about how it came to be where and what it is, what it dreamed of being, and its plans for the future.

66

Rocks

sedimentary	formed by . . .
	examples
igneous	formed by . . .
	examples
metamorphic	formed by . . .
	examples

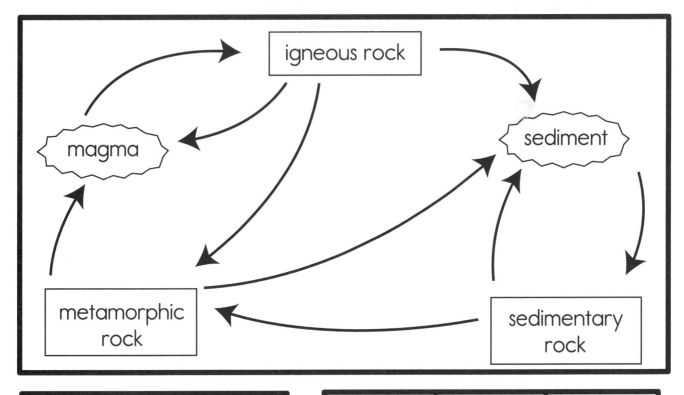

heat and pressure	melting
heat and pressure	melting
	cooling

| weathering and erosion | weathering and erosion | weathering and erosion |
| | | compaction |

Crust Changes

Introduction

Have students describe to partners how objects such as crayons or erasers change over time, focusing on what the changes are and what has caused the changes. Explain that Earth's crust also undergoes changes over time, just like other physical objects.

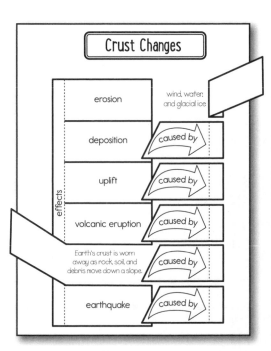

Creating the Notebook Page

Guide students through the following steps to complete the right-hand page in their notebooks.

1.   Add a Table of Contents entry for the Crust Changes pages.

2.   Cut out the title and glue it to the top of the page.

3.   Cut out the flap book. Cut on the solid lines to create six flaps. Apply glue to the back of the left section and attach it to the left side of the page.

4.   Under each flap, describe the effect that process has on Earth's crust.

5.   Cut out the arrow flaps. Apply glue to the back of the right section of each arrow and attach one next to each flap of the flap book so that the left side slightly overlaps the flap.

6.   Under each arrow flap, write what causes the process on the related flap of the flap book.

Reflect on Learning

To complete the left-hand page, have students explain how the following changes could occur:

A. How could a peninsula eventually become an island?

B. How could a new island be formed?

C. How could the surface of a land mass grow?

D. How could a mountain change shape?

E. How could a river's path change?

Crust Changes

effects	
erosion	
deposition	
uplift	
volcanic eruption	
landslide	
earthquake	

caused by

caused by

caused by

caused by

caused by

caused by

Volcanoes and Earthquakes

Introduction

Have students write about natural disasters that pose a threat in their area. What type of natural disaster is most likely to occur (hurricane, tornado, earthquake, etc.)? Have students develop an emergency plan for dealing with that disaster.

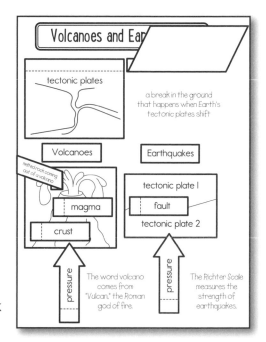

Creating the Notebook Page

Guide students through the following steps to complete the right-hand page in their notebooks.

1. Add a Table of Contents entry for the Volcanoes and Earthquakes pages.

2. Cut out the title and glue it to the top of the page.

3. Cut out the *tectonic plates/fault lines* flap book. Cut on the solid line to create two flaps. Apply glue to the back of the top section and attach it below the title.

4. Write the definition of each term under the flaps.

5. Cut out the *Volcanoes* label and glue it below the *tectonic plates* flap.

6. Cut out the volcano diagram and glue it to the left side of the page below the label.

7. Cut out the *lava*, *magma*, *crust*, and one of the *pressure* flaps. Apply glue to the back of the left sections and attach them to label the diagram.

8. Write the definitions of lava, magma, and crust on the back of the flaps. Write the cause of the pressure that drives the eruption under the *pressure* flap. Below the diagram, write any other notes about volcanoes, such as a description of the Ring of Fire, etc.

9. Cut out the *Earthquakes* label and glue it below the *fault lines* flap.

10. Cut out the diagram of a fault line and glue it on the right side below the *Earthquakes* label.

11. Cut out the *fault* and *pressure* flaps. Apply glue to the back of the left section of the flaps and attach them to the diagram to label the diagram.

12. Write the definition of a fault on the back of the *fault* flap. Write the cause of the pressure under the *pressure* flap. Below the diagram, write other notes about volcanoes, such as a description of the Richter Scale or a list of the possible effects of earthquakes.

Reflect on Learning

To complete the left-hand page, have students draw a Venn diagram to compare earthquakes to volcanoes.

Volcanoes and Earthquakes

tectonic plates	fault lines

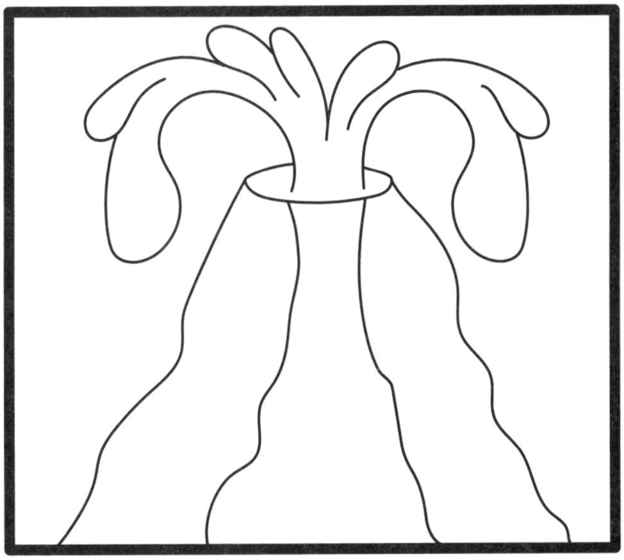

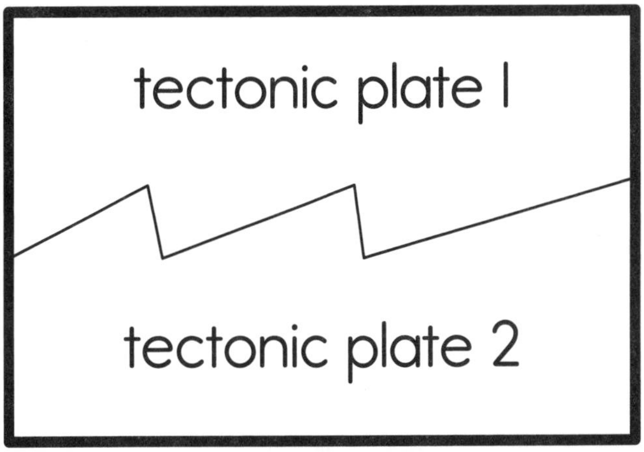

tectonic plate 1

tectonic plate 2

Earthquakes

Volcanoes

lava

magma

crust

fault

pressure

pressure

Formation of Landforms

Introduction

Have students look at pictures of famous landforms. Ask the class to sort the pictures into categories based on what they believe must have created them. Discuss students' reasoning for why they chose to categorize each landform the way that they did.

Creating the Notebook Page

Guide students through the following steps to complete the right-hand page in their notebooks.

1. Add a Table of Contents entry for the Formation of Landforms pages.

2. Cut out the title and glue it to the top of the page.

3. Cut out the *delta*, *canyon*, and *sand dune* flaps. Apply glue to the back of the left or bottom sections and attach them along the left side of the page.

4. Write the definition of each landform under the flap.

5. Cut out the *formed by . . .* piece and glue it below the title on the right side of the page. Cut out the circle flaps. Apply glue to the back of the top sections and attach them on the right side of the page, matching them with the landform they help create. Draw a line to connect the landform flap to each of its circle flaps.

6. Under each of the circle flaps, write how the force on the flap helps contribute to the formation of the landform on the left.

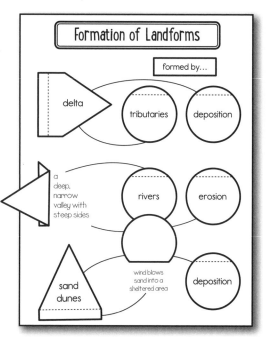

Reflect on Learning

To complete the left-hand page, have students explain what really caused one of the landforms from the introduction.

Formation of Landforms

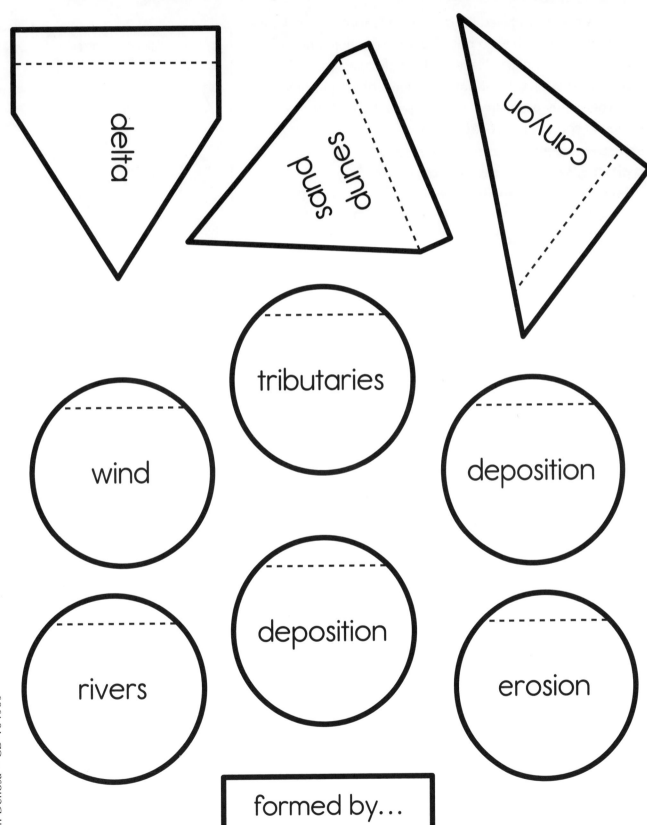

delta

sand dunes

canyon

tributaries

wind

deposition

rivers

deposition

erosion

formed by...

Natural Resources

Have students make a detailed list of their daily routines, making note of not only where they go but what they do there and how they got from place to place. Have students discuss similarities between their schedules. Point out to students different points in their day where they use natural resources (water for brushing their teeth, different sources for electricity, etc.).

Creating the Notebook Page

Guide students through the following steps to complete the right-hand page in their notebooks.

1. Add a Table of Contents entry for the Natural Resources pages.

2. Cut out the title and glue it to the top of the page.

3. Cut out the flap books. Cut on the solid lines to create six flaps on each. Apply glue to the back of the center sections and attach them to the top half of the page.

4. Under the *Where do we find . . .* flaps, write where each natural resource is found. Under the *How do we use . . .* flaps, write how each natural resource is used.

5. Cut out the *Types of Natural Resources* flap book. Cut on the solid lines to create three flaps. Apply glue to the back of the top section and attach it to the bottom of the page.

6. On the top of each flap, define each type of natural resource. Under each flap, write examples of each type of resource. Begin with the examples on the flaps of the flap books above, if you wish. Add other examples as desired.

Reflect on Learning

To complete the left-hand page, have students use the lists they wrote in the introduction to determine what natural resources they use in the course of their everyday lives. Have students label each resource with an *I* for inexhaustible, an *R* for renewable, and an *N* for nonrenewable. Have students brainstorm a list of what they could do to cut down on their use of nonrenewable natural resources.

Natural Resources

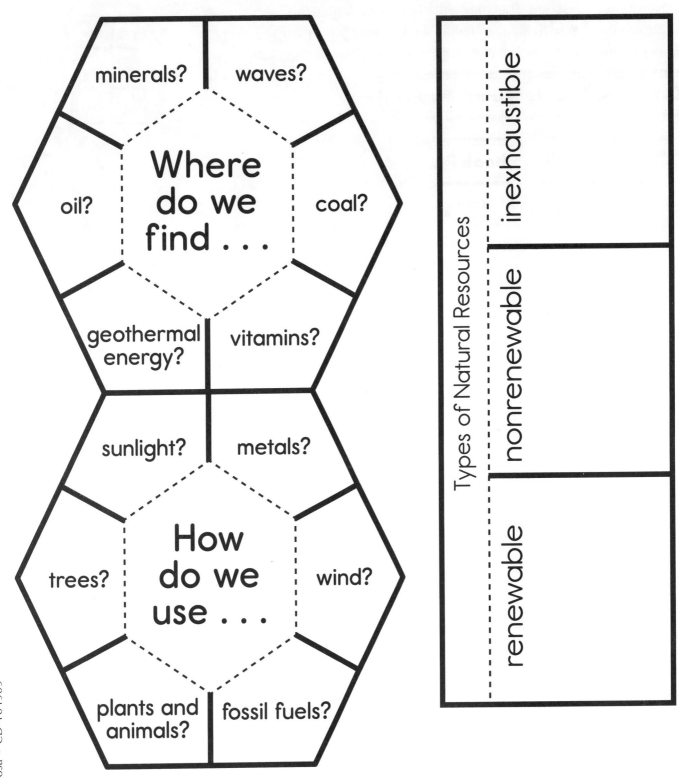

Fossil Fuels

Introduction

Have students describe what they already know about fossils.
What are they? Where are they found? How are they formed?
Connect this to fossil fuels and explain how fossil fuels are formed.

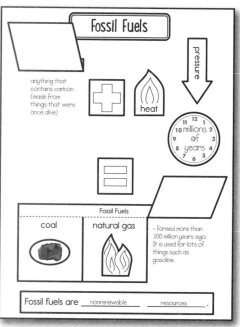

Creating the Notebook Page

Guide students through the following steps to complete the
right-hand page in their notebooks.

1. Add a Table of Contents entry for the Fossil Fuels pages.

2. Cut out the title and glue it to the top of the page.

3. Cut out the *organic matter* flap. Apply glue to the back
   of the top section and attach it to the left side of the
   page below the title.

4. Cut out the plus sign, equal sign, *heat* piece, *pressure*
   piece, and clock. Glue the plus sign to the right of the
   organic matter flap. Glue the *heat* piece, *pressure* piece,
   and clock to the right of the plus sign. Glue the equal sign to the center of the page.

5. On the *organic matter* flap, draw an example of organic matter. Describe what organic matter
   is under the flap. Discuss how with the addition of heat, pressure, and millions of years,
   organic matter is transformed into fossil fuels. Write *millions of years* on the clock to represent
   the amount of time the process takes.

6. Cut out the *Fossil Fuels* flap book. Cut on the solid lines to create three flaps. Apply glue to
   the back of the top section and attach it below the equal sign.

7. Cut out the three pictures. Glue each picture on top of the matching flap of the flap book.

8. Discuss each form of fossil fuel. Under each flap, describe the fossil fuel and how it is used.

9. Cut out the *Fossil fuels are* piece and glue it to the bottom of the page.

10. Complete the sentence. (Fossil fuels are **nonrenewable resources**.)

Reflect on Learning

To complete the left-hand page, have students explain why fossil fuels are not a renewable resource.

Fossil Fuels

organic matter

heat

pressure

Fossil Fuels		
coal	natural gas	oil

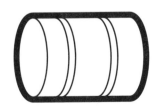

Fossil fuels are _____ _____ .

Tabs

Cut out each tab and label it. Apply glue to the back of each tab and align it on the outside edge of the page with only the label section showing beyond the edge. Then, fold each tab to seal the page inside.

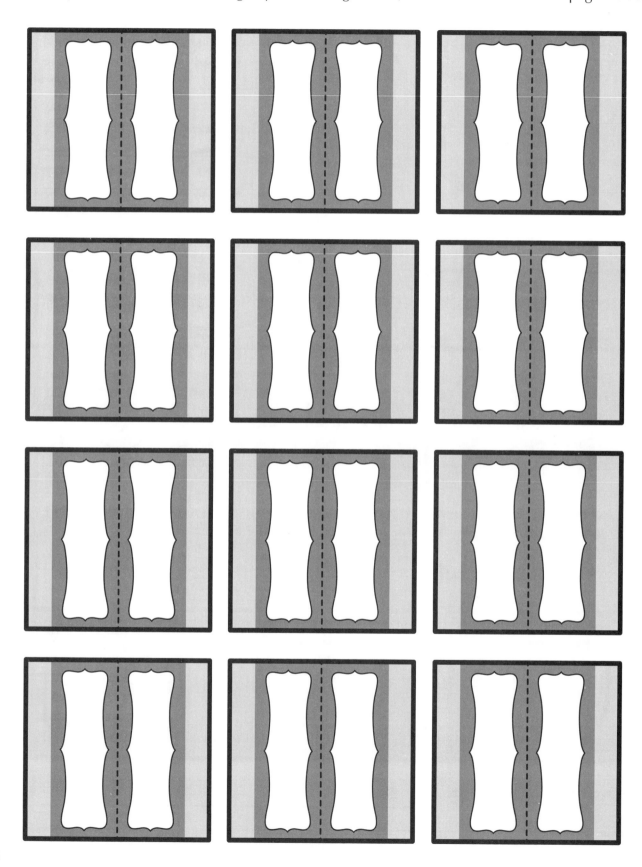

Cut out the KWL chart and cut on the solid lines to create three separate flaps. Apply glue to the back of the Topic section to attach the chart to a notebook page.

What I

Know

What I

Wonder

What I

Learned

Topic: _____

Library Pocket

Cut out the library pocket on the solid lines. Fold in the side tabs and apply glue to them before folding up the front of the pocket. Apply glue to the back of the pocket to attach it to a notebook page.

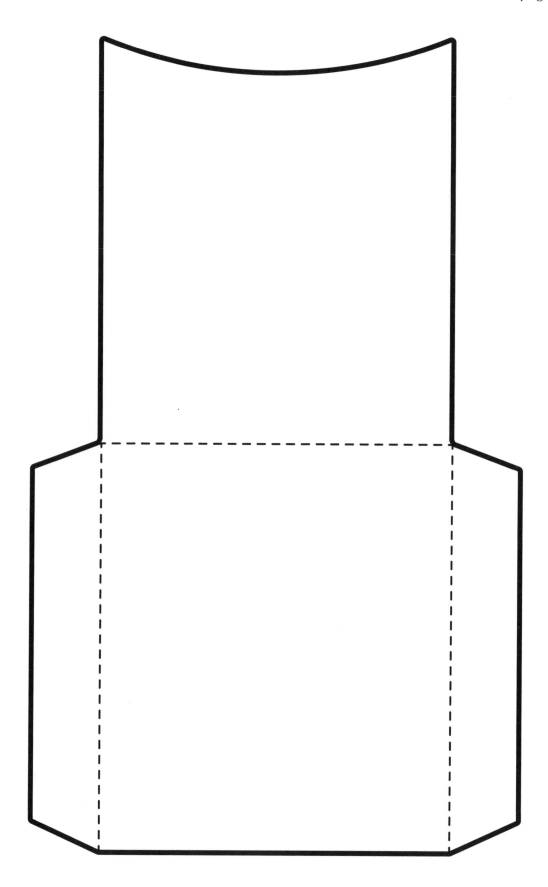

Envelope

Cut out the envelope on the solid lines. Fold in the side tabs and apply glue to them before folding up the rectangular front of the envelope. Fold down the triangular flap to close the envelope. Apply glue to the back of the envelope to attach it to a notebook page.

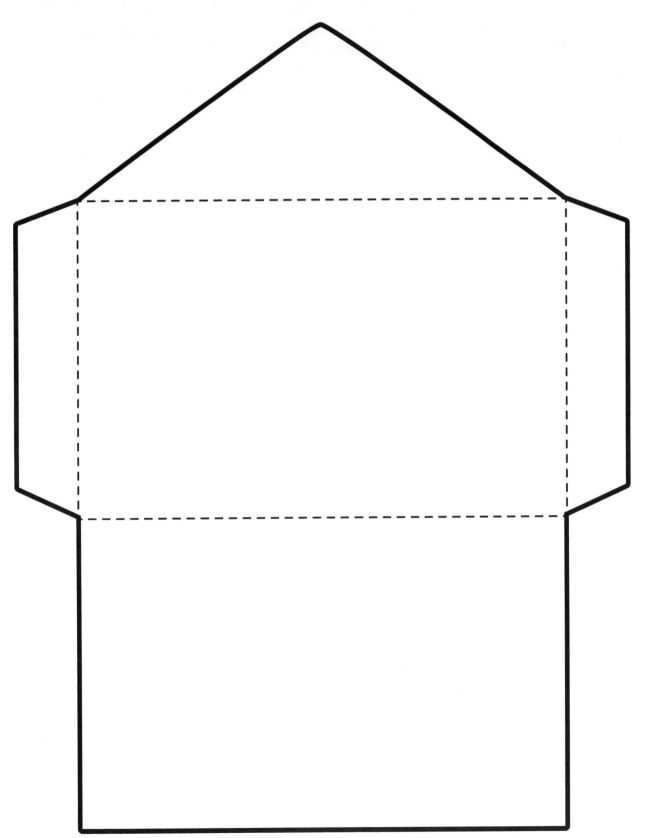

Pocket and Cards

Cut out the pocket on the solid lines. Fold over the front of the pocket. Then, apply glue to the tabs and fold them around the back of the pocket. Apply glue to the back of the pocket to attach it to a notebook page. Cut out the cards and store them in the envelope.

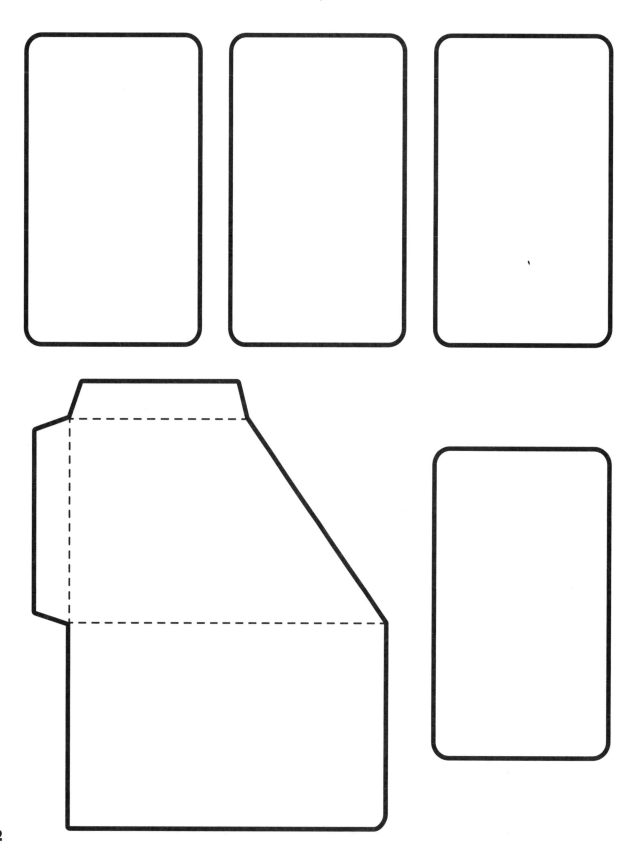

© Carson-Dellosa • CD-104909

Six-Flap Shutter Fold

Cut out the shutter fold around the outside border. Then, cut on the solid lines to create six flaps. Fold the flaps toward the center. Apply glue to the back of the shutter fold to attach it to a notebook page.

If desired, this template can be modified to create a four-flap shutter fold by cutting off the bottom row. You can also create two three-flap books by cutting it in half down the center line.

Eight-Flap Shutter Fold

Cut out the shutter fold around the outside border. Then, cut on the solid lines to create eight flaps. Fold the flaps toward the center. Apply glue to the back of the shutter fold to attach it to a notebook page.

If desired, this template can be modified to create two four-flap shutter folds by cutting off the bottom two rows. You can also create two four-flap books by cutting it in half down the center line.

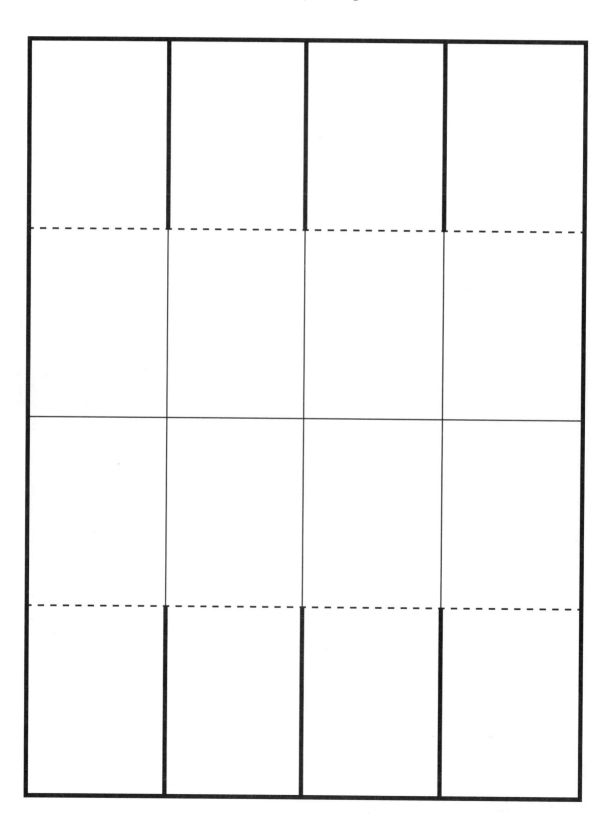

Flap Book—Eight Flaps

Cut out the flap book around the outside border. Then, cut on the solid lines to create eight flaps. Apply glue to the back of the center section to attach it to a notebook page.

If desired, this template can be modified to create a six-flap or two four-flap books by cutting off the bottom row or two. You can also create a tall four-flap book by cutting off the flaps on the left side.

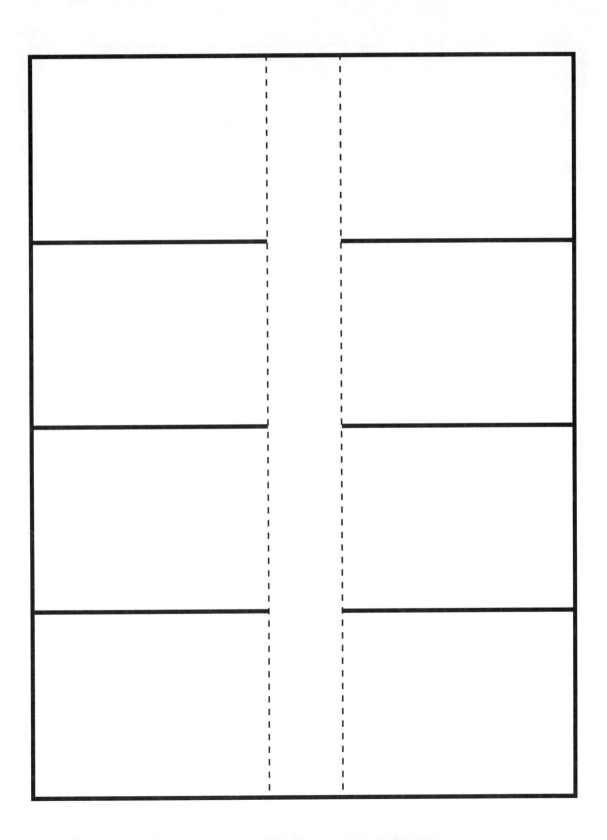

Flap Book—Twelve Flaps

Cut out the flap book around the outside border. Then, cut on the solid lines to create 12 flaps. Apply glue to the back of the center section to attach it to a notebook page.

If desired, this template can be modified to create smaller flap books by cutting off any number of rows from the bottom. You can also create a tall flap book by cutting off the flaps on the left side.

Shaped Flaps

Cut out each shaped flap. Apply glue to the back of the narrow section to attach it to a notebook page.

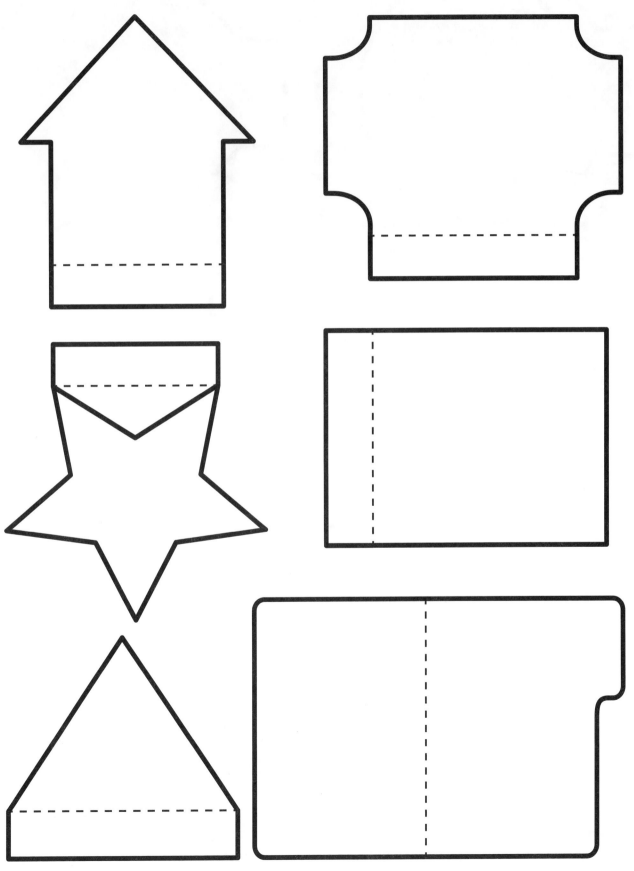

Shaped Flaps

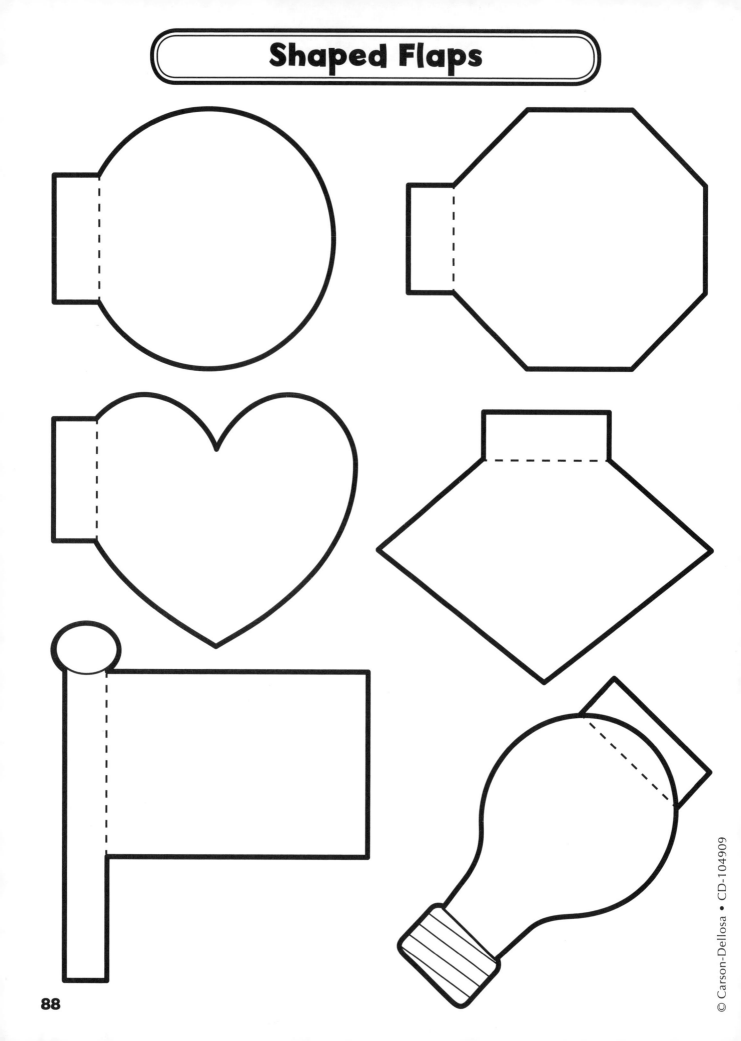

Interlocking Booklet

Cut out the booklet on the solid lines, including the short vertical lines on the top and bottom flaps.
Then, fold the top and bottom flaps toward the center, interlocking them using the small vertical cuts.
Apply glue to the back of the center panel to attach it to a notebook page.

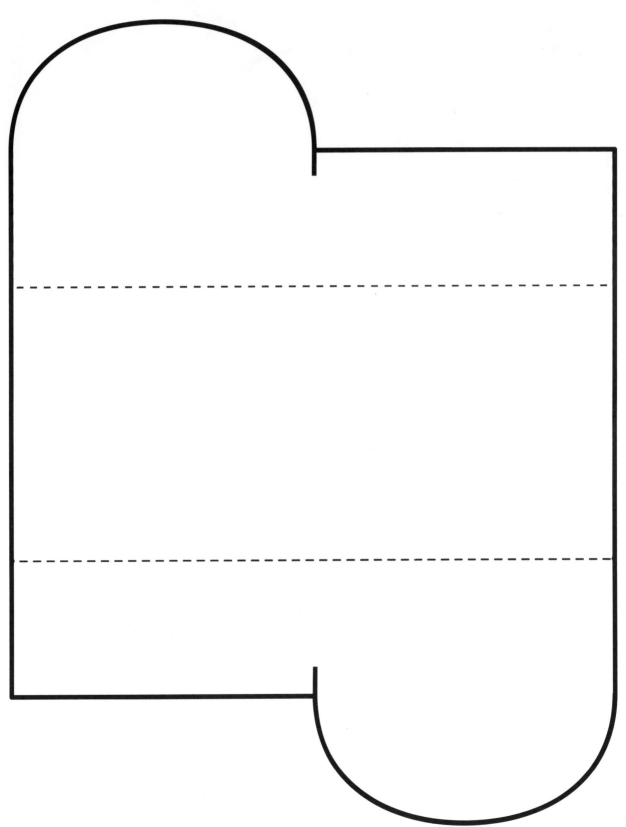

Four-Flap Petal Fold

Cut out the shape on the solid lines. Then, fold the flaps toward the center. Apply glue to the back of the center panel to attach it to a notebook page.

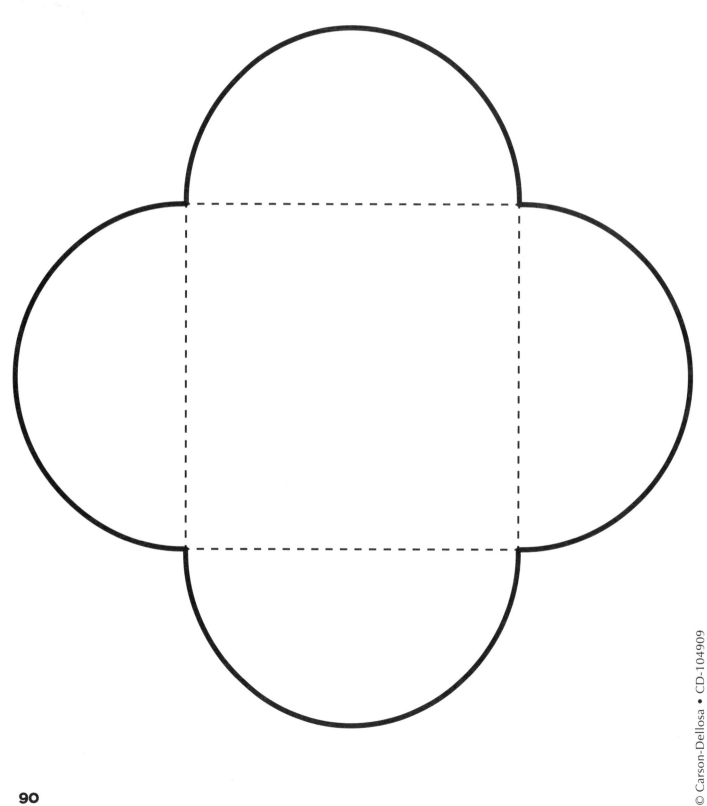

Six-Flap Petal Fold

Cut out the shape on the solid lines. Then, fold the flaps toward the center and back out. Apply glue to the back of the center panel to attach it to a notebook page.

Accordion Folds

Cut out the accordion pieces on the solid lines. Fold on the dashed lines, alternating the fold direction. Apply glue to the back of the last section to attach it to a notebook page.

You may modify the accordion books to have more or fewer pages by cutting off extra pages or by having students glue the first and last panels of two accordion books together.

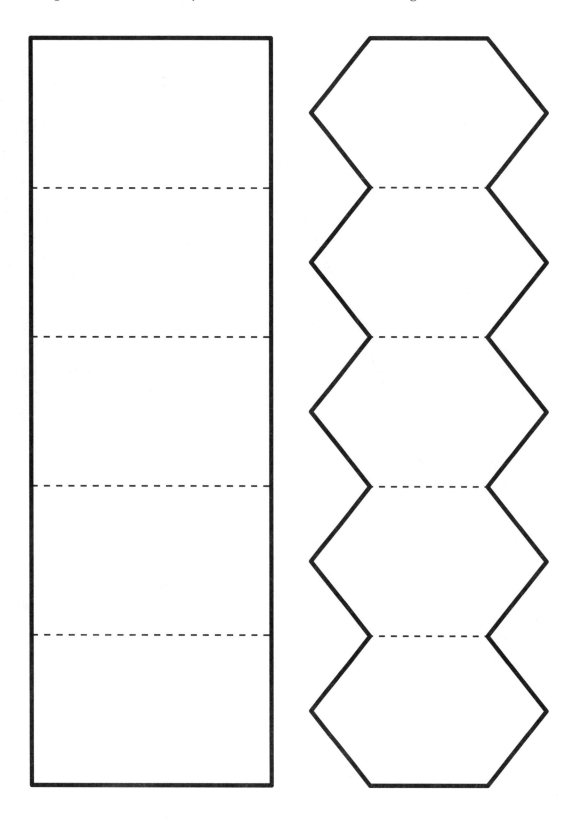

Accordion Folds

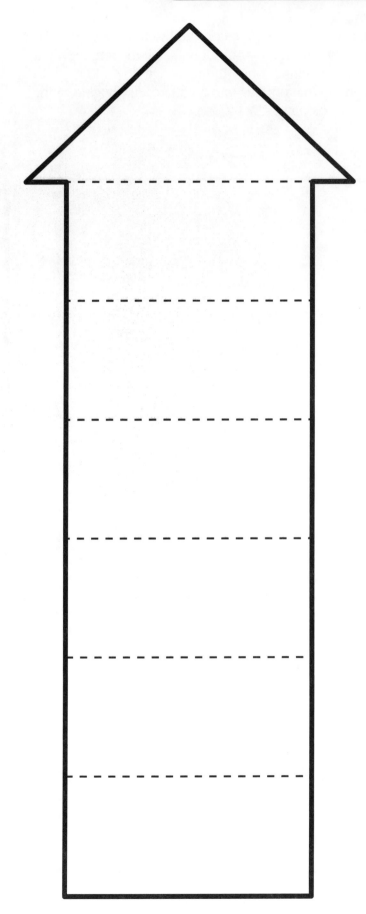

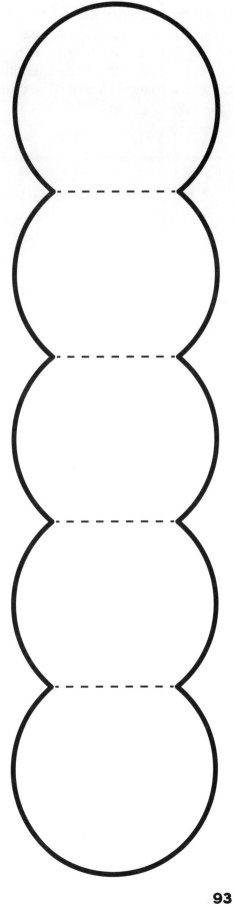

Clamshell Fold

Cut out the clamshell fold on the solid lines. Fold and unfold the piece on the three dashed lines. With the piece oriented so that the folds form an X with a horizontal line through it, pull the left and right sides together at the fold line. Then, keeping the sides touching, bring the top edge down to meet the bottom edge. You should be left with a triangular shape that unfolds into a square. Apply glue to the back of the triangle to attach the clamshell to a notebook page.

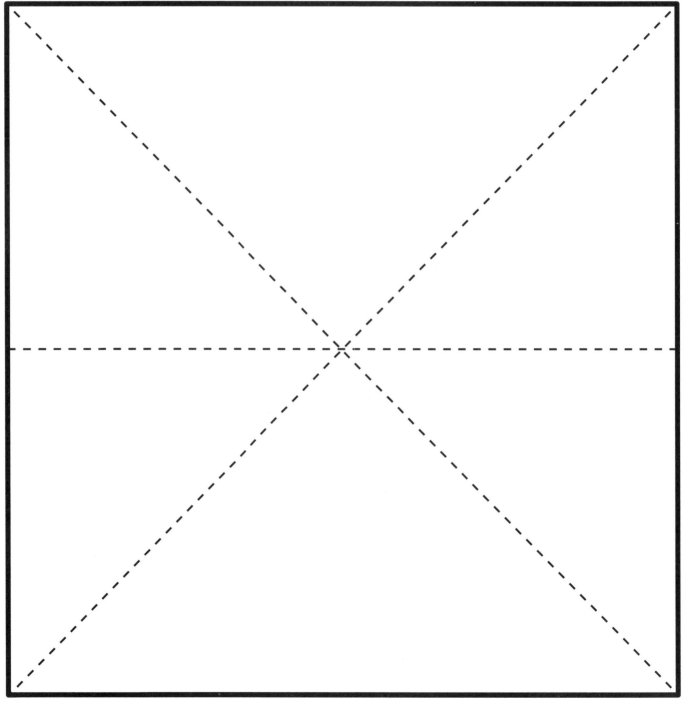

Puzzle Pieces

Cut out each puzzle along the solid lines to create a three- or four-piece puzzle. Apply glue to the back of each puzzle piece to attach it to a notebook page. Alternately, apply glue only to one edge of each piece to create flaps.

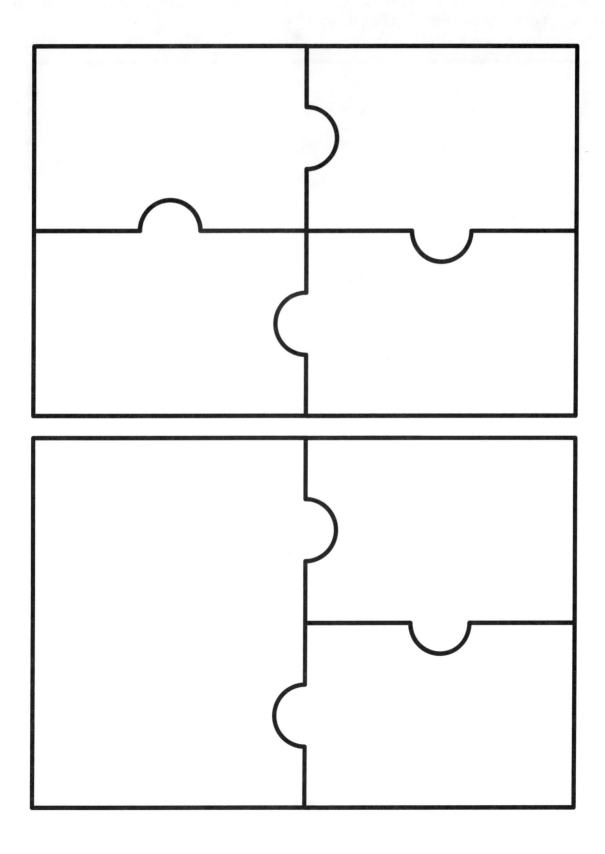

Flip Book

Cut out the two rectangular pieces on the solid lines. Fold each rectangle on the dashed lines. Fold the piece with the gray glue section so that it is inside the fold. Apply glue to the gray glue section and place the other folded rectangle on top so that the folds are nested and create a book with four cascading flaps. Make sure that the inside pages are facing up so that the edges of both pages are visible. Apply glue to the back of the book to attach it to a notebook page.

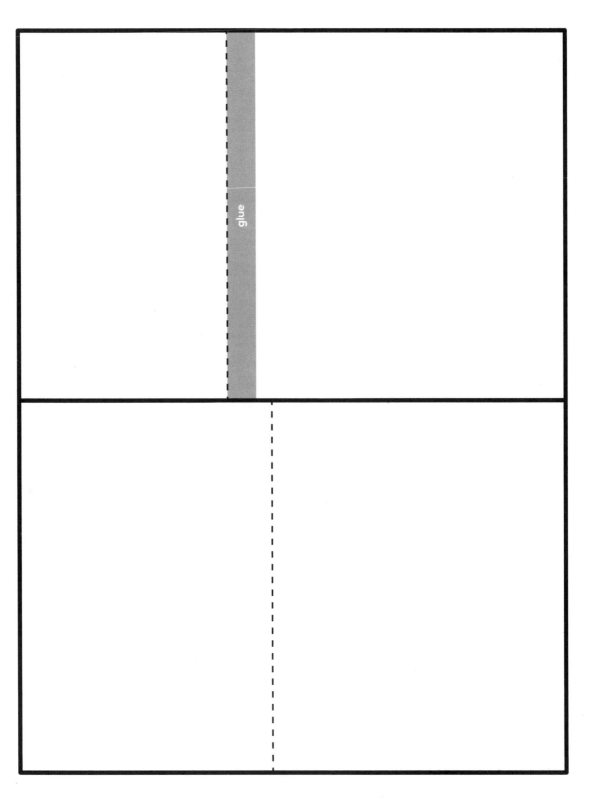

glue